W9-ADF-663

They're Playing Our Song

A NEW MUSICAL COMEDY

BOOK BY *Neil Simon*

MUSIC BY *Marvin Hamlisch*

LYRICS BY *Carole Bayer Sager*

RANDOM HOUSE · NEW YORK

To Manny Azenberg, Robert Moore, George Rondo,
Pat Birch, Tharon Musser, Lani Sundsten, Doug Schmidt,
Ann Roth, Bob Currie, Larry Blank, and Phil Cusack

THEY'RE PLAYING OUR SONG *was first presented in New York on February 11, 1979, by Emanuel Azenberg at the Imperial Theatre, with the following cast:*

VERNON GERSCH	Robert Klein
SONIA WALSK	Lucie Arnaz
VOICES OF VERNON GERSCH (BOYS)	Wayne Mattson, Andy Roth, Greg Zadikov
VOICES OF SONIA WALSK (GIRLS)	Helen Castillo, Celia Celnik Matthau, Debbie Shapiro

Directed by Robert Moore

Musical Numbers Staged by Patricia Birch

Scenery and Projections by Douglas W. Schmidt

Costumes by Ann Roth

Lighting by Tharon Musser

Music Direction by Larry Blank

Orchestrations by Ralph Burns, Richard Hazard, Gene Page

SYNOPSIS OF SCENES

ACT ONE

SCENE 1: Vernon's Apartment—Central Park West, New York City

SCENE 2: Vernon's Studio—Five Days Later

SCENE 3: Le Club

SCENE 4: Sonia's Apartment—An Hour and a Half Later

SCENE 5: On the Street

SCENE 6: On the Road

SCENE 7: A Beach House in Quogue, Long Island

ACT TWO

SCENE 1: Vernon's Apartment—A Few Days Later

SCENE 2: Vernon's Bedroom—Three Weeks Later

SCENE 3: Vernon's Bedroom—The Middle of the Night

SCENE 4: A Recording Studio—Eleven O'Clock the Next Morning

SCENE 5: A Hospital Room—Los Angeles—A Few Months Later

SCENE 6: Sonia's Apartment—A Few Months Later

MUSICAL NUMBERS

ACT ONE

Overture

"Fallin'"	VERNON
"Workin' It Out"	VERNON, SONIA, VOICES
"If He/She Really Knew Me"	SONIA, VERNON
"They're Playing Our Song"	VERNON, SONIA
"If She/He Really Knew Me" (Reprise)	VERNON, SONIA
"Right"	SONIA, VERNON, VOICES
"Just for Tonight"	SONIA

ACT TWO

"When You're in My Arms"	VERNON, SONIA, VOICES
"I Still Believe in Love"	SONIA
"Fill in the Words"	VERNON, VOICES

Act One

*A grand piano is onstage. A single spotlight is directed at it.
At the piano is* VERNON GERSCH, *about thirty-four. He wears
slacks, sports shirt, cardigan sweater, loafers.*

*He is playing a melody. A soft, sweet melody. He hums along
with it, composing. He writes the music down on a sheet in front
of him.*

*The doorbell rings. He is lost in his music. It rings again. With
the pencil in his mouth and the sheet of music paper in his
hand, he crosses to the door and opens it.*

SONIA WALSK *comes in. Late twenties, attractive, although her
clothes belie that fact. She dresses like a cross between Annie
Hall and a gypsy tea reader. She carries a large shoulder bag
and a leather portfolio.*

SONIA   Hi. Sonia Walsk. I tried to time it right, but I'm about
ten minutes early.

VERNON   (*Pencil in mouth*) I'll be right with you. Sit down.

SONIA   I am really *soo* delighted—
(*He goes back to piano and sits. He plays a few more
bars and jots down his work. She sits and takes in the
apartment, almost afraid to glance at him for fear of dis-
turbing him. He finishes the musical phrase, then
quickly gets up and crosses to her*)

VERNON   Hello. Vernon Gersch.

SONIA   (*Jumps up*) Hi. Sonia Walsk. I tried to time it right, but
I'm about ten minutes early. I am really *soo* delighted—

VERNON   Actually you're twenty minutes late, but no problem.
Can I take your jacket?

SONIA   I'm not wearing one. It's all part of the dress.

VERNON   Ahh. Very fashionable.

SONIA   No. Just thrifty. (*Gasps*) Oh, God. I can hardly catch
my breath.

VERNON   You didn't *walk* up, did you?

SONIA No. I'm just nervous. Didn't you notice when I shook your hand? It was a little clammy . . . mine, not yours . . .

VERNON Did I do something to make you nervous?

SONIA Yeah. You won two Grammies and an Academy Award.

VERNON Oh? I'm sorry.

SONIA It's not your fault. (*She picks up the Oscar*) They're lighter than I thought.

VERNON They're chocolate on the inside. Would you like a drink? Some coffee? Coke?

SONIA I used to go to a shrink in this building.

VERNON No kidding? Me too. That's how I found this apartment.

SONIA Dr. Tannenbaum?

VERNON Dr. Markle.

SONIA I went to Tannenbaum.

VERNON He died last summer. Tannenbaum.

SONIA I didn't know . . . If you went to the funeral, he'd probably charge you for the hour. (*Looks out the window*) Nice view of the park.

VERNON I never look. I'm afraid of heights.

SONIA Then wasn't the fourteenth floor a mistake?

VERNON Except I always wanted to live in this building. Famous for musicians. Jerome Kern was one of the first tenants. Isaac Stern lived here. Leonard Bernstein. Where do *you* live?

SONIA West Eighteenth Street. Famous for poverty. Mostly artists. They keep painting pictures in the halls, I can never find my door. I wish I could afford something like this . . . Do you enjoy having money? Am I being too nosy?

VERNON No, no. You've been here almost three minutes . . . Sure I do. Well, not the money, but the things that come with it.

3

SONIA Well, I have all the things that *don't* come with it, and it stinks. Like having to buy my clothes secondhand. This is from *The Cherry Orchard*.

VERNON I don't know that store.

SONIA It's not a store. It's a play by Chekhov. My girl friend wore it in the Brooklyn Academy production. It's practically new. She only wore it for thirty-eight performances and six previews.

VERNON You're lucky they didn't go out on tour.

SONIA I got my eye on a terrific dress that's in *Dracula*. It's all white with little black bats, perfect for New Year's Eve. (*Looks at the sheet music on piano*) How'd you like my lyrics?

VERNON Your lyrics?

SONIA You had them all weekend. Didn't you read them?

VERNON Oh. Yes. For a minute I forgot why you were here. I was very involved with the *Dracula* dress . . . Listen, I have to be very honest with you. You don't look at all like what I expected.

SONIA What do I look like?

VERNON You're very pretty. I didn't expect someone very pretty.

SONIA Oh? You mean you found my lyrics unattractive?

VERNON I found them unhappy. A little sad. I expected someone very pale with a giant teardrop hanging from each eye.

SONIA When I write, it brings out my serious side. You'll notice I never wear anything from *Hello, Dolly!*

VERNON I never thought pretty girls had major problems.

SONIA They do when they turn thirty. That's for starters. Then I gave up smoking. *And* I just broke up with the fellow I was living with. I called my mother for the first time in a year and a half, and before I could say hello, she says, "Are you still fat?" . . . And I'm in hock to my publisher for eight hundred dollars because I went to Tiffany's and bought myself a ring to celebrate my not committing suicide at turning thirty. So I guess I write sad songs.

VERNON   Well, they're damn good. I really like your lyrics.

SONIA   Well, we're batting a thousand because I really like your music.

VERNON   Naturally, not *all* your lyrics.

SONIA   I wouldn't expect you to. I know how high your standards are . . . How many did you like?

VERNON   One.

SONIA   That many?

VERNON   *Part* of just one.

SONIA   I can live with that . . . Let me guess—"Fallin' "?

VERNON   Yes. Well, obviously you know that's the best.

SONIA   It's not the best, but it suits your style the best.

VERNON   Oh? You find my style somewhat limited?

SONIA   Not at all . . . I think you have great range. Great . . . unexplored range . . . Did that come out wrong?

VERNON   Only if you happen to hear it.

SONIA   What I mean is . . . Well, what I like about your music is that it's so fundamentally basic, so intrinsically melodic, so universally embraced . . . Oh, God, I just don't want to use the word "commercial."

VERNON   But I take it you do want to write popular songs. I mean, we're not here to write the score for *The Gulag Archipelago.*

SONIA   Oh, God. Yes. I've only had one hit in my whole life. That's why I want to write with you.

VERNON   Good. I've been working on a tune this morning. You might find it intrinsically melodic.
     (*Crosses to piano*)

SONIA   I heard something weird about you.

VERNON   What?

SONIA   Well, there was a rumor that you were engaged to three different girls last year. Is there any truth to it?

VERNON   Yes.

SONIA   (*Shrugs*) Some people think everything is weird. If you're planning anything new, I've got this ring up for sale.

VERNON   Thank you. I buy them by the gross. Listen, some of these lyrics are very clever. Very Dorothy Parker. Personally, I don't go for things like "Let's play two sets in Massachusetts," but I admire the skill.

SONIA   I wrote that when I was eleven. If you have a tune you wrote when you were eleven, maybe we could do something with it.

VERNON   Would you settle for a melody to "Fallin'"? I just finished it.

SONIA   My God, you mean we wrote our first song together? I wish I knew, I would have dressed for the occasion.

VERNON   No, no. *The Cherry Orchard* is fine. Before I start, are you sure you don't want something to eat?

SONIA   I wouldn't want to be indebted to you in case I don't like the music.

VERNON   Listen, we'd better settle that right now. You have to be completely honest with me. I'm a mature person. I have an ego, but I can take criticism. If you don't like it, you *must* tell me . . . It won't happen with *this* song because this one is fabulous . . . But please feel free to speak up. (*He sets up the music. She walks over to the window and looks out*) Don't you want to sit here? You can hear it better.

SONIA   I don't listen with my ears.

VERNON   You don't? You found some other interesting part of the body in which sound enters?

SONIA   (*Taps her chest*) I listen in here . . . with the soul.

6

VERNON   I see . . . Well, I don't have a big voice, so could you
turn your soul this way, please. (*He starts to play the intro*)
This is very rough, you understand.

SONIA   I didn't expect to get it on the charts by tonight.
(*He nods, takes a deep breath and sings "Fallin'"*)

VERNON

    I'm afraid to fly
    And I don't know why.
    I'm jealous of the people who
    Are not afraid to die.
    It's just that I recall
    Back when I was small
    Someone promised that they'd catch me
    And then they let me fall.

    And now I'm fallin'
    Fallin' fast again.
    Why do I always take a fall
    When I fall in love?

    You'd think by now I'd learn
    Play with fire, you get burned.
    But fire can be oh so warm
    And that's why I return.
    Turn and walk away
    That's what I should do.
    My head says go and find the door
    My heart says I found you.

    And now I'm fallin'
    Fallin' fast again.
    Why do I always take a fall
    When I fall in love?

    It always turns out the same—
    Loving someone, losin' myself.
    Only got me to blame.

    Help me, I'm fallin'
    Fallin'
    Catch me if you can.

Maybe this time I'll have it all
Maybe I'll make it after all
Maybe this time I won't fall
When I fall in love.

> (*He finishes the song gently, letting the last note linger, then drops off into silence. She still has her back turned to him, staring out the window . . . He waits patiently. Finally she turns and looks at him*)

SONIA   It's good. I like it.

VERNON   "It's good, you like it"? Try to control your enthusiasm. I wouldn't want you to froth at the mouth . . . I think it's *fantastic!*

SONIA   You told me to be honest. Some of it is lovely. Some *not* so lovely.

VERNON   Which part didn't you like?

SONIA   The lyrics.

VERNON   The *lyrics?? You* wrote the lyrics. Didn't you ever hear them before?

SONIA   Not with the music. The music is too good for the lyrics. It's beautiful. It made me cry. I would like to write you a different lyric.

VERNON   I don't *want* a different lyric. I *love* this lyric. I heard the music in my head the minute I read them. I would like to keep this lyric.

SONIA   Oh, God, Vernon, you are so gifted. I feel so inadequate. I can't write. I'm a fake, a fraud. I just put down anything. The first thought that pops into my mind. It's high school garbage. I don't know what the hell I'm doing in this business. I should be running a day-care center somewhere.

VERNON   You're not having a breakdown, are you? Tannenbaum is dead. Maybe you could see Markle?

SONIA   You mean you *really* like it? I have to know, Vernon. *The truth!*

VERNON Yes. I like it. I think it's a first-rate song.

SONIA Because I have such respect for your talent. That's why I was so nervous coming up here today. I put this dress on backward. I don't know if you noticed.

VERNON Look, will you please stop telling me I make you nervous. Because it makes me nervous. I'm just plain Vernon Gersch. Not Mozart. Not Beethoven.

SONIA Oh, but you are. How sweet that you don't realize how good you are. Your music is as important to *your* time as their music was to theirs. My God, you can't sit in a dentist's chair without hearing one of your songs. I think you're truly gifted. I think you are our only, our *only* contemporary living American composer.

VERNON Well, thank you. That's very kind.

SONIA Maybe Stephen Sondheim.

VERNON Steve is good. I love Steve's work.

SONIA And if you say to me you don't want me to touch those lyrics, then I will not touch those lyrics.

VERNON Please . . . don't touch those lyrics.

SONIA Well, then would you think about the first eight bars of the music? Somehow it doesn't work for me. (*She looks at her watch*) Oh, God. I have to run . . . I don't know how to fix it. That's your department. Listen, I'm not going to tell Mozart or Beethoven how to write . . . I'm having all my hair cut off in an hour. You think I'm wrong? I trust your opinion. If you think I shouldn't have it cut off, I will not have it cut off.

VERNON At this moment my feeling is, cut off anything you want.

SONIA I respect your advice. I really enjoyed this session. It was very productive. When do you want to work again? I'm completely free and clear.

VERNON Well, we should get started soon. I promised Barbra we'd have five songs by the eighteenth.

SONIA   No problem. I write quickly. Monday morning, ten A.M. sharp?

VERNON   (*Writes in his datebook*) Sharp it is. Meet me at my studio. 111 East Tenth Street. It's more relaxing there. See you Monday.

SONIA   Oh, Monday's bad. Make it Tuesday.

VERNON   All right. Tuesday at ten.

SONIA   Make it ten-thirty.

VERNON   Swell.

SONIA   Eleven is better.

VERNON   I already changed it.

SONIA   I'm going to the Hamptons for the weekend. Wow, this is really a great opportunity for me, Vernon. I thank God and our agents for putting us together. I'll make you proud of me, I swear. You inspire me like no one I've ever worked with. (*She shakes his hand vigorously*) If you get those first eight bars fixed, you can call me at Gurney's Inn, East Hampton. I think you can up the tempo a little, too. It's a little draggy. But you'll work it out. Have a nice weekend.

> (*And she is out the door. He stands there, numbed by his experience*)

VERNON   A little *draggy* . . . She's out of her mind.

> (*At the piano, he plays. Lights fade. She is out in the hall. She stops, sings*)

SONIA

God, he's such a genius
When he played I almost cried.
Imagine telling him
How his music should begin.
I'm gonna write this weekend
And forget about Gurney's Inn.
Next time he'll like me
Next time my dress will be on straight
I'll set my watch an hour fast
And I won't be late!

VERNON's *studio. Midmorning five days later. It is a gray, rainy day. An occasional clap of thunder.*

VERNON *appears, new sweater and shirt. He crosses impatiently to window, looks out, then looks at his watch. He crosses back to tape machine and presses the record button. He picks up hand mike.*

VERNON (*Into mike*) Journal. Wednesday, May 17, eleven-twenty A.M. A date remarkable only in the fact that Sonia Walsk is now one day and twenty minutes late. The one day I could write off to eccentricity. It's the twenty minutes that *bugs* me . . . I have further concern for the future of our collaboration because of certain personality conflicts. She's a flake. And I'm a flake. Two flakes are the beginning of a snowstorm . . . Also of major consideration is that I can't stand working with people who just gave up smoking. (*The doorbell rings*) Doorbell at eleven twenty-two. I am showing signs of hives. (*Doorbell again, impatiently*) She rings impatiently. No doubt to put *me* on the defensive.

(*She pounds on the door with her fist*)

SONIA Open the door, for God's sake!

VERNON (*Into mike*) Suddenly Godzilla's outside. To be continued.

(*He presses off button, puts down mike. He crosses to the door and opens it.* SONIA *rushes in, wearing another one of her "dresses"*)

SONIA Where's your bathroom?

VERNON Listen, I think you and I have to get a couple of things straight around—

SONIA (*Standing on a throw rug*) If this is an expensive carpet, you'll tell me where your bathroom is.

VERNON In there, first door on your left. (*She rushes off. He goes back to tape machine, presses "on" button and picks up mike*) Eleven twenty-four. No attempt at explanation. She went directly to the toilet. She is wearing another one of those

11

dresses that seem to cry out, "Enter Olga Petrovka from stage right" . . . There is no doubt in my mind that collaboration is an ugly business. No wonder the word fell into disrepute during the Second World War.

(SONIA *comes back in*)

SONIA Whew! I just made it.

VERNON (*Into mike*) Thank God! (*He clicks it off*) Listen, I think you and I have to—

SONIA Who's N.K.G.?

VERNON N.K.G.?

SONIA Those are the initials on the hand towels.

VERNON Natalie Klein. One of the girls I was engaged to. She kept all the gold and silver gifts, I got everything terry cloth . . . Does it bother you that it's twenty after eleven?

SONIA Yes, I know. I'm late. I'm sorry. It's raining, I couldn't get a cab.

VERNON It wasn't raining yesterday when you were supposed to be here.

SONIA I had a rough weekend. I broke up with Leon. He's the fellow I was living with.

VERNON You told me that on Thursday.

SONIA I went back with him on Friday. I thought I'd give it one more chance. I don't give up easily on relationships.

VERNON That's encouraging to know in case we get as far as this afternoon.

SONIA I said I was sorry. It will never happen again. I will even try to go to the bathroom before I get here. Beyond that, I don't know what else to say.

VERNON Is that the dress from *Dracula?*

SONIA No. It's from *Of Human Bondage.*

VERNON The movie?

SONIA   The play. They revived it in Dallas.

VERNON   And you didn't cut your hair?

SONIA   No. Leon talked me out of it. He likes it long.

VERNON   (*Puzzled*) You still like to look good for the man you just broke up with?

SONIA   I can't stand his possessiveness, but I respect his taste.

VERNON   Well, I can only hope you and I begin as well as you and Leon ended. (*He crosses to piano*) Now, then . . . There was another song you left that first day. "Workin' It Out." I think I have an idea for something.

SONIA   "Workin' It Out"? Oh! Well, I'm glad you liked the lyric.

VERNON   I don't. I just like the title.

SONIA   (*Shrugs*) I'll take what I can get.

VERNON   I'm not quite sure where the song goes yet. (*He starts to vamp*) I hear some funky disco beat. Get 'em all nuts at Studio 54 . . . Real low-down, you know, like—
    (*He sings*)
Ooh, workin' it out . . . la la la la la la la la
Workin' it out . . . la la la la la la la la
Workin' it out . . . la la la la la la la

SONIA   (*Yells*) Hey! Whoa! Wait a minute! Hold it! Hold it! Save your la la la la's— (*He stops playing*) You can't come that fast at me. I'm a lyricist, not an IBM computer. I don't work that way.

VERNON   No? How do you work?

SONIA   I have to think about it. I deal in words. Thoughts. Ideas. Images. I have to sit down all by myself in a nice comfortable chair with a pad and a pencil and then I—
    (*She catches herself and stops*)

VERNON   And then you what?

SONIA   Well, I have this peculiar way of working. I talk it out with the girls.

13

VERNON   What girls?

SONIA   The other Sonias. The voices. The ones in my head. (*Shrugs*) The girls.

VERNON   (*Nervously*) You mean there's an entire *group* of you?

SONIA   Yes. In a way.

VERNON   All dressed like that?

SONIA   I guess. They're the other sides of my personality. We *all* have them. None of us is just one person. We have—ego. We have passion. We have skepticism.

VERNON   Are those their names?

SONIA   No. They're all Sonia. Just like you have other Vernons . . . Do you ever talk to yourself?

VERNON   A lot. When I'm waiting for you.

SONIA   Well, the one who's listening is another Vernon. When you write music and you can't hit that top note, who sings it in your head? When you're writing melody, who sings the harmony?

VERNON   (*Thinks*) The *boys?*

SONIA   Exactly.

VERNON   Why didn't you say so? I thought you were talking about somebody else. Now, can we get back to the song? (*He vamps*) See if you and the girls can come up with something . . .
   (*He sings "Workin' It Out"*)
Ooh, workin' it out
La la la la la la la la la
Workin' it out
   (*Speaks*)
You'll put in some lyrics here.

SONIA
   The last thing I need to hear today
   Is a melody.

VERNON
　La la la la la la

SONIA
　I'm findin' out
　Nobody gives you their songs
　For free.

VERNON
　La la la la la la

SONIA
　He wants one thing
　He wants another
　I just wanna run and take cover.
　I need a little more time
　Just for me.

VERNON
　Can't you see I'm workin' it out

SONIA
　Workin' it out
　That's what I'm tryin' to do.
　Workin' it out

VERNON
　Dance for me, baby

SONIA
　For Leon, for me and you.
　Workin' it out

GIRLS
　It should be easy to do

SONIA
　But you never had to work it out

GIRLS
　You never had to work it out
　You never had to work it out

VERNON　(*Speaks*) Work it out!

SONIA
> Work it out for two.

VERNON   (*Speaks*) Listen, I think it could be like a Bee Gees record here. You know, about broken hearts or something like—

SONIA
> Look at the way he works.
> What would he know of a broken
> Heart?

VERNON	GIRLS
Do it for me, mama!	Ah . . .
	and

SONIA *and* GIRLS
> To him "broken heart" is a phrase
> I should write for his goddamn
> Middle part.

VERNON   (*Speaks*) You'll fill it in here.

SONIA	GIRLS
He's askin' me for	
words that are clever.	Ooh . . .
Leon and me	
We had five years together.	
I need a little more time	

GIRLS
> Time!

SONIA
> Just for me

GIRLS
> Can't he see

SONIA
> I'm workin' it out

VERNON
> Workin' it out

SONIA

    You gotta give me a chance.
    Just 'cause I hear your music

VERNON

    Baby

SONIA

    Don't mean I gotta dance.

SONIA	GIRLS
Workin' it out—	
It should be easy to do	It should be easy
But you never had to	
work it out	

VERNON   (*Speaks*) Work it out!

SONIA

    Work it out for two.

VERNON   (*Speaks*) Here's where my boys come in—

VERNON *and* BOYS

    La la la la la la la la la la la la
    La la la la la la la la la la la la
    La la la la la la

GIRLS

    Gotta give him something.

VERNON

    Hey, baby

SONIA

    He took my lyric
    Kept my title
    Threw out every word.

VERNON *and* BOYS

    Baby, ah . . .

SONIA

    He made some crazy disco thing.
    It's not at all the song I heard
    But—

GIRLS
> Maybe his way's better.

SONIA
> Who knows?
> I'm too unclear.

SONIA *and* GIRLS
> Right now my mind's in such a mess,
> I hardly know I'm here.

VERNON *and* BOYS
> Hey, baby, la la la la la la
> La la la la la la
> La la la la la la

GIRLS
> Gotta find a lyric

SONIA
> Gotta give him something.

VERNON *and* BOYS
> La la la la la la
> La la la la la la

GIRLS
> Tell him you don't like it.

VERNON *and* BOYS
> Hey, baby

SONIA	BOYS
If someone else had written this	
I'd know just what to say.	Baby, ah . . .
I'd say it's not my kind of song,	
Can't we write something Else today, but	

GIRLS
He might get insulted.

BOYS
La la la la

SONIA
His ego isn't small.

BOYS
Baby

GIRLS
If you don't write him something quick

SONIA *and* GIRLS
We might not work at all

VERNON *and* BOYS
Don't you know that I'm
Workin' it out
Workin' it out
La la la la la la la la la la la la

SONIA *and* GIRLS
I've got to work it out

VERNON *and* BOYS
Workin' it out
Workin' it out
La la la la la la

SONIA *and* GIRLS
Help me work it out

BOYS
Bye, bye, baby

VERNON   (*Speaks*) The music is great. Now it's on you.

SONIA
I'll try even harder
That's all I can do.
But you never had to work it out

VERNON   (*Speaks*) Let's go to work!

SONIA

Work it out for two.

BOYS *and* GIRLS

Workin' it out, workin' it out
La la la la la la la

VERNON Anyway, that's the general idea . . . What do you think? About the song? . . . Hello? . . . Anything coming from the soul?

SONIA Listen, Vernon. I think we have to sit down and have a serious talk.

VERNON As opposed to all our gay, witty conversations of the past?

SONIA How do you expect me to work with you if I don't even know who you are? Every time I walk in the door, you rush off to the piano. Why don't we just sit, talk, get to know each other?

VERNON Because when I'm sitting here and talking, you're out somewhere breaking up with Leon.

SONIA Leon is gone. Out of my life. Now I'm sitting and talking. Tell me about yourself. About your family, about school, about music, about what it really feels like to be Vernon Gersch.

VERNON Look, you don't just *divulge* your entire personality. It's like toothpaste. It comes out a little bit at a time.

SONIA So how come I'm having trouble getting your cap off?

VERNON Look, if we don't work I'll have enough time to write my autobiography, and then you'll know everything about me.

SONIA (*Not giving up*) How old were you when you started playing the piano?

VERNON (*Disgruntled*) Four-and-a-half.

SONIA And you didn't keep falling off the stool?

VERNON No. They tied me to a coatrack.

SONIA   Did you ever have a desire to write really serious music? Like an opera?

VERNON   Yes! I wish I were doing it *right now!*

SONIA   Look, I think the problem is we're trying to get to know each other in a working atmosphere. I think the two of us have to get out and loosen up a bit.

VERNON   Are you suggesting a gym?

SONIA   I'm suggesting we meet somewhere in a more relaxed setting . . . I think it might be helpful if we had dinner together.

VERNON   Heavy! Very heavy suggestion! I have never dated anyone I ever worked with . . . man *or* woman.

SONIA   Who said anything about a date? I just said dinner. Dinner isn't necessarily a date.

VERNON   Oh! You mean a *business* dinner.

SONIA   No! That's our problem *now!* I don't want to discuss business. I want to have a nice sociable dinner.

VERNON   *That's a date!*

SONIA   A date is when two people get together socially in hopes of getting together again even more socially . . . I want to get together socially in hopes of getting together again so we can *work!*

VERNON   You know, talking to you is like sending out your laundry. You never know what the hell is coming back! All right! I'll do it. I don't even want to know what it is . . . a dinner, a date. Surprise me!

SONIA   Good. Thank you . . . I think having a nice casual dinner can be enormously helpful, and I appreciate your making this effort.

VERNON   It's my pleasure . . . How about tomorrow night?

SONIA   I'm busy tomorrow.

VERNON   My shirts just came back without buttons.

SONIA   Leon and I see our therapist tomorrow night.

VERNON   I thought you broke up with him.

SONIA   We'd like to split without any bitter feelings and we need help. So we're seeing a doctor.

VERNON   (*Shrugs*) Well . . . it makes just as much sense as the date *we're* having. How about the night after?

SONIA   Can't. It's Leon's birthday. I'm giving him a small party.

VERNON   Look, you want to wait a few years until the breakup is firm and then try again?

SONIA   It's over *now*. I am feeling guilty about it. *I'm* the one who walked out. I don't intend to see him after the party . . . I can have dinner with you tonight.

VERNON   Fine. Should I make a reservation for three?

SONIA   Believe it or not, I really can handle my life very well. I just have trouble with the people who can't handle theirs . . .

VERNON   Well, up to now, I've been doing a bang-up job with mine, thank you. I'll make a reservation.
   (*He crosses to phone*)

SONIA   You think I'm bizarre, don't you?

VERNON   (*Picks up phone, dials. To* SONIA) Well, in this business I think we're all a little rococo. (*Into phone*) Hello. Is Fernando there? . . . Vernon Gersch . . . Yes, I'll hold.
   (*She sings "If He Really Knew Me"*)

SONIA
   If he really knew me
   If he really truly knew me
   Maybe he would see the other side of me
   I seldom see.
   If there were no music
   If his melodies stopped playing
   Would he be the kind of man
   I'd want to see tonight?

Does the man make the music
Or does the music make this man
And is he everything I thought he'd be?

If he really knew me
If he'd take the time to understand
Maybe he could find me
The part I left behind me
Maybe he'd remind me of who I am.

VERNON (*Into phone*) Thanks, Fernando. (*He hangs up. To* SONIA) Eight-thirty. Ever been to Le Club? Or is that too dressy?

SONIA No. Terrific. I can finally get to wear my outfit from *Pippin*. Bye.
    (*And she is gone.* VERNON *moves to his tape recorder and clicks it on*)

VERNON Eleven thirty-six . . . She's gone. Pulse rate normal again . . . Evaluation of Sonia Walsk. On positive side, she is extremely bright, speaks with candor and honesty, has enormous energy and enthusiasm . . . On the negative side, she is extremely bright, speaks with candor and honesty, enormous energy and enthusiasm . . . In short, this girl's a lot to deal with.
    (*He sings "If She Really Knew Me"*)
If there were no music
If my melodies stopped playin'
Would I be the kind of man
She'd want to see tonight?

What the hell—it's just a dinner.
If this doesn't work—that's it!
And can I really be so hungry for a hit?

If she really knew me
If she'd take the time to understand
Maybe she would find me
The part I left behind me
Maybe she'd remind me
Of who I am.

Le Club.
Soft, sexy disco music in the background. On the walls, we see
the flickering shadows of dancers moving to the music.

VERNON *is sitting alone at a table, a bottle of wine in front of*
him and two glasses. He looks at his watch and drums his fingers
on the table impatiently.

VERNON   This is not happening to me . . .

SONIA   (*Rushes in, in* Pippin *outfit*) I know. I'm late. I couldn't
help it. I'm sorry. What is it, a quarter to nine?

VERNON   Ten to ten.

SONIA   Were you bored?

VERNON   No, they were playing a lot of Elton John . . . In fact
all of Elton John.

SONIA   (*Sits down*) I don't blame you for being angry. I had a
terrible scene with Leon. He doesn't want to break up. He
wants me to come back. I couldn't get him out of my apartment. He was hysterical when I left. If I ever needed proof
I'm doing the right thing, tonight was it . . . Oh, God, I'm
famished.

VERNON   Shall we order dinner?

SONIA   The thing is, I don't think I can stay. I'm really scared
about leaving him alone. When he gets like this, he's capable
of doing anything.
(VERNON *grabs wine bottle, wants to hit her*)

VERNON   Well, I'm glad you dropped by . . . Maybe we can get
to know each other one course at a time. A shrimp cocktail
one night, a mixed green salad another . . .

SONIA   Do you think I'm overreacting?

VERNON   I don't know. Was Leon in the tub holding himself un-
derwater?

SONIA Maybe I should just let him thrash it out up there. The thing is, he just refuses to accept our separation. Has anything like this ever happened to you?

VERNON I once changed my insurance man and he stopped sending me calendars. Nothing worse than that.

SONIA What about those three girls you were engaged to?

VERNON I wasn't really. The first girl was an actress who just liked to get her name in the papers. When you dialed her number, it also rang at the New York *Post* . . . Then there was Tina. We dated three times. Unfortunately her father was a caterer and very quick with announcements.

SONIA And then came Natalie Klein.

VERNON Well, Natalie was different.

SONIA How?

VERNON I'd rather not discuss it.

SONIA *I* told you about Leon. Why won't you tell me about Natalie?

VERNON Because I choose not to. Next subject, please.

SONIA Well, off to another great start, aren't we?

VERNON *I* started. You came in in the middle.

SONIA Is that why you're so belligerent?

VERNON Look, lady. I didn't suggest this. I told you it was dangerous. I thought it was better if we stayed in the apartment and wrote our five songs and nobody would get hurt.

SONIA *Lady??* That's a snide thing to say.

VERNON (*Turns away*) Oh, Jesus.

SONIA That's a really chauvinistic remark. Why did you call me "lady"?

VERNON Because I had two genders to pick from and I took a chance on the feminine. If I made a mistake, I'm sorry, Chuck.

SONIA   That's as denigrating as if I called you "boy." How about writing a few songs, *boy?*

VERNON   (*Looks around, embarrassed*) Will you lower your voice? Everyone is looking. I came here for dinner, I turned out to be the floor show.

SONIA   Is that why you don't want to talk about Natalie? Is that where all your hostility toward women comes from?

VERNON   (*Calmly*) Check! May I have the check, please? . . . Somebody?

SONIA   Are you *leaving?* The minute we're beginning to get somewhere?

VERNON   We haven't gotten past the first five minutes of *any* of our three meetings. It doesn't bode well for our future. (*Calls out*) Waiter! Can I find a waiter here who's on my side?

SONIA   Don't go, please. At least we're bringing things up to the surface. I think there's something here worth fighting for.

VERNON   (*Rises*) The Thirteen Colonies were worth fighting for . . . *Israel* is worth fighting for. Nowhere in our brief history can I find a reason for bearing arms. (*Yells off*) Do you want my lousy money or not?

SONIA   (*Gets up*) Dance with me.

VERNON   What?

SONIA   I want to dance. Forget what I said. Forget everything. Let's just have a good time . . . Come on, Vernon, let's get it on.

VERNON   I can't change moods that quickly.

SONIA   Yes, you can. Don't hold on to your anger. (*She dances invitingly*) Let it all come out with the music . . . Come on . . . Dance with me.

VERNON   To the Bee Gees? Why should I push *their* record? (*But he sees it's no use and she does seem so inviting. He gets up and they dance to slow, sensual rock . . . He is extremely awkward. As they dance*) I'm a lousy dancer.

26

SONIA   Some things don't have to be said. (*He starts to walk away . . . She grabs him and pulls him back*) I find it attractive.
(*They resume dancing*)

VERNON   That I can't dance?

SONIA   Now I know you can't do everything. I'm not so in awe of you . . . And I find that attractive.

VERNON   I also can't ski and I can't swim. You must be *nuts* about me now.

SONIA   Not yet . . . but give a girl a chance.
(*He looks at her with renewed interest . . . They dance closer . . . She smiles*)

VERNON   What are you smiling about?

SONIA   You're fingering my back like you're playing the piano.

VERNON   Oh. Sorry. I was working.

SONIA   You mean you were composing on my spinal column?

VERNON   I just wrote eight bars on your lower lumbar region.

SONIA   Well, don't write any concertos. We're in a public place.

VERNON   (*Smiles*) You know, for a dumb idea . . . maybe this wasn't such a dumb idea.
(*They look at each other. Their eyes connect. And for the first time, something even deeper connects between them . . . Suddenly she breaks away and goes back to their table*)

SONIA   I'm sorry . . .
(*She sits*)

VERNON   What's wrong? What did I say now?

SONIA   It wasn't you. It was Leon.

VERNON   (*Looks*) Is he here?

SONIA   I tell *you* not to hold on to your anger, but *I'm* the one who can't let go of the past . . . It's crazy, I know. Here I am enjoying myself for the first time in months and suddenly (*He sits*) I'm feeling guilty because Leon is so despondent. I've always been like that. If I got an A in history and my best friend got a C, I would go home in tears. (*The music changes*) I feel personally responsible for the happiness of people I care about. I went to an analyst I hated for two years because I didn't want to hurt his feelings . . . I remember one time—

(VERNON *holds up his hand for her to be quiet*)

VERNON Shh. Listen.

SONIA What is it?

VERNON Don't you hear what they're playing? Don't you recognize it? That was my first really big hit . . . three years ago this month.

SONIA *What?*
(*He sings "They're Playing My Song"*)

VERNON

Ho, ho, they're playin' my song
Oh, yeah, they're playin' my song
And when they're playin' my song
Everybody's gotta shh shh shh.

Don't say a word now.
Listen to that sweet melody.
I'm happy to say
In my own humble way
Every perfect note of that was written by me.

Ah, ha, they're playin' my song
That table's humming along.
That couple half out the door
Is coming back to hear
More of my music.
At first I thought this place was a dive.
I chose it in haste
But they showed they got taste
As long as they're playin' my song.

Who would have known nine months ago
That I would give birth at my piano?
In all honesty I've got to admit
I knew this song would be an international hit.

Ah, ha, they're playin' my tune
Too bad it's ending so soon.
But when we all gotta go
It's good to know that
They'll be playin'
Oh, God, I'm prayin'
They'll be playin'
They'll be playin' my song.
    (*He finishes and sits down. He looks at her*)
I'm sorry. You were saying . . . ?

SONIA   (*Slightly aghast*) Do you *always* do that?

VERNON   Certainly. Don't you?

SONIA   Well, I get a thrill if I'm in a restaurant or an airplane and I hear one of my songs, but I don't get up in the aisle and stop lunch.

VERNON   It's been my dream since I was a kid. To walk into a club with Ingrid Bergman on my arm, the band spots me and plays all of my hits, and Ingrid looks at me adoringly and says, "I'm so lucky" . . . What was *your* dream?

SONIA   To go up and win a Grammy and not feel guilty about my friends who didn't.

VERNON   Well, maybe that's the difference between us. I don't get insane if people like or don't like me . . . as long as they like my music.

SONIA   You're lucky.

VERNON   Except for Natalie Klein. She was crazy about me. Hated my music. It drove me nuts. She would tear my clothes off in Grand Central Station. But in bed, I'd put on one of my tapes and she'd switch it to Alice Cooper.

SONIA   I can see why you called it off.

VERNON When I told her it was over, she got hysterical. She said she would *force* herself to like my music. The ultimate put-down, right? Then one day last summer we were driving out to Bridgehampton and I happened to say—

SONIA (*Holds up one hand*) One second.

VERNON What is it?

SONIA What is it? It's my big one. Last summer, it's all they played. Talk about taking off—
    (SONIA *sings "They're Playing My Song"*)

SONIA
    Ho, ho, they're playin' my song.
    Oh, yeah, they're playin' my song.
    And when they're playin' my song
    Everybody's gotta shh shh shh.
    The magic of words
    Is weavin' its spell round this room.

    Nobody's dancin'
    They're all too entranced in
    Just listenin' to the perfect way
    My words fit that tune.
    Right now they're listenin' to me.
    My lyric reads like a poem.
    It surely stands on its own.

    It makes me proud to hear that music.
    It's a total expression of me.
    To be more specific
    This place is terrific
    As long as they're playin' my song.

    Who would have known two years ago
    When Leon asked, "Can't lovin' be fun?"
    Who would have known "Can't Lovin' Be Fun"
    Would be sung by everybody under the sun?

    You know this made the top ten.
    All good things come to an end.
    I wish they'd play it again and again.

Let 'em keep on playin'
Oh, God, I'm prayin'
They'll be playin' my song.
Ho, ho, they're playin' my song.

VERNON   Oh, yeah, they're playin' your song.

SONIA
I wish they'd play it again and again.
Let 'em keep on playin'
Oh, God, I'm prayin'
They'll be playin' my song.
    (*Speaks*)
You're right. That feels wonderful. I have to do that more
often . . . Oh, God, you were talking about Natalie Klein. I
am sorry. Go on.

VERNON   That's okay. I enjoy not talking about her. Would you
believe I'm beginning to enjoy talking to you?

SONIA   Aha! A smile! A small victory for Sonia Walsk.

VERNON   No, no. I had my teeth cleaned today. I didn't want to
waste it.

SONIA   Gee, it suddenly got—friendly in here.

VERNON   I must be maturing. If I met you in college, you would
have scared the hell out of me.

SONIA   I know. It's a problem. I have a tendency to come on
full-steam-ahead.

VERNON   That's why I always rush behind the piano . . . to get
out of the way . . . Did you wear that perfume the first day
we met?

SONIA   Yes.

VERNON   Funny. I didn't smell it till tonight.

SONIA   It's on a time-release. It goes to work when things begin
to click.

VERNON   Oh? . . . Are we clicking?

SONIA Well, you're not running and you're not hollering . . .
So to me, that's clicking.

VERNON You know, you have an incredible energy that's hard
to resist. I have the feeling if there were a blackout in the city,
you would be the only thing still lit up.

SONIA You should see my electricity bills . . . You know, it's
nice to see you finally coming out from behind the Steinway.

VERNON It's a Yamaha. I got a break in the price.
*(They look at each other a moment. A romantic ballad
is playing underneath)*

SONIA My God! I've just spent five minutes without worrying
about Leon . . . You know, when I first walked in your door—

VERNON Wait a minute! . . . Listen to what they're playing.

SONIA *(She listens)* Is that one of *your* songs?

VERNON No.

SONIA It's not one of mine . . . Nice romantic ballad . . .
What is it?

VERNON I don't know what it is, but I know what it's going to
be.

SONIA *and* VERNON
Oh, they're playin' our song
Yeah, they're playin' our song

VERNON
I really like you tonight.

SONIA
Ev'rybody, please—

BOTH
Shh . . .

SONIA
This man is a master.
His music . . .

VERNON
Her words are . . .

BOTH
Divine.
We started out shaky
But we've broken the ice.
On a bottle of wine,
Well, you seem twice as nice.

SONIA *I'm* ready to work. Your place, ten o'clock tomorrow morning?

VERNON What's wrong with *your* place tonight? I suddenly have an overwhelming passionate desire to compose.

SONIA (*Looks at him*) Sure. Why not? (*He quickly gets up, helps her up. She stops*) We can't. Leon is still there.

VERNON (*Angrily*) Why don't you and I break up so we can spend more time together? . . . We'll go to my place!

SONIA No. Be at my place in an hour. (*She takes out an eyebrow pencil and writes it on the tablecloth*) Here's my address. If I don't get Leon moved out tonight, I never will.

VERNON And what if you never will?

SONIA Then I'll be the dumbest girl in New York. (*She runs off, stops, turns*) Better make it an hour and a half.
(*She goes off. He takes off the tablecloth and folds it up and puts it in his pants pocket, most of it hanging out*)

VERNON Well, listen, if she thinks I'm going to spend the rest of my life waiting to hear how the continuing saga of Sonia and Leon is going to be resolved, she picked herself the wrong boy. I'm not something you rent at Avis, you know, where you can just pick me up and leave me when you want . . . This whole experience has left me so depressed, I don't know if I can work any—
(*Music starts to play—*VERNON *sings*)
Ho, ho, they're playin' my song.
Oh, yeah, they're playin' my song.
And when they're playin' my song
Ev'rybody's gotta shh shh shh—
(VERNON *exits*)

Her apartment.
An hour and a half later.
It is a small, sloppy and shoddy apartment. She is wearing a robe, sitting on the sofa, wiping her teary eyes.
The doorbell rings.

SONIA   (*Glumly*) It's open.
(VERNON *walks in very cautiously, looks around for* LEON)

VERNON   Hi! Any casualties?

SONIA   It's okay. He's gone.

VERNON   So is last winter, but it's coming back.

SONIA   I don't ever want to go through a scene like that again. He walked out of here so determined he was going to make it on his own. He had the sweetest look on his face. Like a twelve-year-old boy going off to camp for the first time.

VERNON   It's a picture I'll remember forever.

SONIA   I'm sorry. I left you standing there. Please come in. Close the door, sit down.

VERNON   Is this where you live?

SONIA   Certainly. What did you think it was?

VERNON   Very charming.

SONIA   It's a dump.

VERNON   I find dumps charming.

SONIA   Somehow I could never find a reason for fixing it up. Bespeaks of the relationship, don't you think?

VERNON   Not necessarily. You could eat off my mother's floor and my father didn't speak to her for thirty years.

SONIA   Would you like a drink? A glass of wine?

VERNON   I'd better not. We forgot to have dinner during dinner.

34

SONIA   You must be starved.

VERNON   I'm okay. (*Takes a handful of tidbits from cocktail dish*) Oh, I love these. Those little pebble candies.
(*He puts a few in his mouth*)

SONIA   No. They're just pebbles. I collect them.
(*He spits them out in his hand*)

VERNON   You ought to put a sign up. A person could get gallstones.

SONIA   You must think I'm an awful slob.

VERNON   No, no. Call it "artistic license."

SONIA   It's strange. But the only place I have orderliness in my life is with my lyrics. I have six months of unwashed laundry in the bathroom, but I'll spend four weeks looking for the right word in a song.

VERNON   Why don't you write in the bathroom? Get them both done together.

SONIA   I'm glad you're here, Vernon. I really needed someone to talk to.

VERNON   Well, my intentions were other than verbal, but—I'm all ears . . . Well, maybe not *all*.

SONIA   (*Turns away, more tears*) Damn! I'm sorry.

VERNON   No, *I* am. I didn't mean to be glib. I'm beginning to see the side of you that isn't *Hello, Dolly!*

SONIA   I am soo *dumb!* I've been trying to break up with the man for six months, and now that he's gone it's so painful. How did you say goodbye to Natalie Klein?

VERNON   I'm not good at confrontations. I left a message on her service. (*This manages a smile from her*) Look, maybe this is the wrong time for me to—

SONIA   No, please don't go. I have such mixed emotions about what I've done. And I feel this enormous need to just talk it out.

35

VERNON Wouldn't your analyst be better than a composer?

SONIA He's in Mexico getting divorced . . . All I need is a friend sitting in a chair . . . I was wondering if—well, no. That's silly.

VERNON What?

SONIA . . . Would you mind sitting in for him?

VERNON For your *analyst?*

SONIA You wouldn't have to do anything.

VERNON I can barely get *myself* through the day.

SONIA You wouldn't have to say anything. I just want you to listen. That's all *he* does. I listen to myself talk and then figure out things for myself. That's why he's such a good doctor.

VERNON No wonder mine stinks. He's always giving me advice.

SONIA If you're tired, you can even doze off.

VERNON Really? Do you have any movie magazines?

SONIA Gee, I really appreciate this. (*She moves a chair to the sofa*) You sit here, I'll be on the sofa.
(*She lies down on the sofa*)

VERNON What are you doing? You're not going to lie down? I mean, that's really *official!*

SONIA I don't have to, if it makes you uncomfortable.

VERNON Well, I wouldn't want a malpractice suit . . . Go ahead, lie down.
(*She does*)

SONIA (*Takes a deep breath*) Well, let's see . . . Where shall I begin?

VERNON I feel I should have a pipe in my mouth.

SONIA You have to be quiet. Otherwise I can't think.

VERNON Sorry.

SONIA Well, Leon and I had been living together close to five years now . . . I've known him almost *ten* years. We met back in—

VERNON (*Looks at watch, whispers*) Excuse me. What time did we start?

SONIA That's not important. Just listen.

VERNON Sorry.

SONIA We met back at college. At Middlebury. He was in the band. I was editor of the school paper.

VERNON Yes, I know.

SONIA (*Turns around*) How do you know that?

VERNON Well, I assume you would have told me all that in previous sessions.

SONIA No, no. Don't actually be my doctor. It's not going to get *that* confidential. Let me talk and you just listen, okay?

VERNON Sure. That's easy . . . Hell of a way to make a living.

SONIA (*Lies back down again*) Anyway, everything was fine for a while . . . And then, I don't know, the last year or so I've felt this need to be more . . . (*He keeps saying "Mm hm"*) . . . independent, to be out on my own . . . We were still writing together, but it just wasn't as good as it was in the beginning . . . So I began working with some other composers, had a few hits, I recorded some, played a few clubs . . . Please don't keep saying "Mm hm." It's very distracting. Okay?

VERNON Mm hm . . . Sorry!

SONIA I was nervous going out in front of a lot of people, but the exhilarating thing was this feeling of being in control of my own life. Once you step out there, you're all alone . . . and if you can cut that, you can cut anything . . . Well, it was just a few weeks ago I decided I was going to sever the umbilical cord forever . . . and that's about when I met you.

VERNON   Is "me" Vernon or the doctor?

SONIA   *Vernon!* You're always *Vernon.* The doctor is in Mexico.

VERNON   Gotcha. Just wanted to get it straight. Go on. This is fascinating.

SONIA   As I said, that's when I met you . . . and I don't know, there was something different about you . . . a little intimidating . . . I'm always concerned with what you're thinking about . . . and I like that . . . (*Music sneaks in*) . . . Because it means I have to come up with the goods. I like challenges.

   (*She continues her speech and* VERNON *sings softly "If She Really Knew Me"*)

VERNON	SONIA
If she really knew me If she really truly knew me Maybe she would see the Other side of me. I hide of me. If there were no music If my melodies stopped playin' Would I be the kind of man She'd want to see tonight?	. . . I had a contemporary American literature teacher in Middlebury. He had two eyes that could burn a hole right through me. He knew I had some talent, but he wasn't going to let me get away with anything. I really didn't like him, but I tried harder for that man's approval than anyone I ever met before . . . He gave me an A-plus for the course, and on graduation day he said to me, "You got through by the skin of your teeth, Walsk. You'd better shape up" . . . That's what you make me do. Shape up . . . Oh, Jesus, I'm suddenly feeling very self-conscious.

SONIA   I'm sorry. This was a stupid thing to do. Can we stop now?

VERNON   Now? You still have forty-five minutes on your session.

SONIA   I keep saying I want to get to know you, and I'm the one who's always doing the talking . . . How about *you* lying down for a while?

VERNON   Oh, I gave that up. I'm into self-analysis now.

SONIA   You mean you analyze *yourself?*

VERNON   Mondays and Fridays, five to six.

SONIA   Are you serious?

VERNON   It saves a lot of time. I trust myself. I have a lot of confidence in me. I can open up and not be ashamed to hear what I have to say.

SONIA   I don't believe you.

VERNON   I swear. I'm really making some major breakthroughs. The only trouble is I have to stop soon. I go on vacation in August.

SONIA   Come on, Vernon. What are you avoiding?

VERNON   I'm not avoiding anything.

SONIA   What is it you're so afraid to find out about yourself?

VERNON   I'm not afraid . . . I don't know. I've always had this theory that all great talent is an outgrowth of some deep-seated neurosis. And that if I were completely secure and happy, I wouldn't be able to write music any more . . . For example, there's a place in Russia where these smiling, happy yogurt-eating farmers live to be a hundred and forty years old . . . But there's not one of them who has a song in the top forty . . . and that's since before Christ.

SONIA	VERNON
If he really knew me	I'm much more an instinctual
If he'd take the time	person than analytical. If I
To understand	started to analyze where it
Maybe he could show me	came from or how it got there,
Maybe he could find me	the well would probably dry
Maybe he'd remind me of	up and little droplets of music
Who I am.	would *drip drip drip* until my

brain would crack and turn to parchment . . . There are some things in life that just shouldn't be analyzed. Like making love. I don't want to know *why* it feels nice to stroke a girl's hair or touch her skin. I just want to stroke and touch. Let her worry about why I'm doing it. I got enough troubles just getting her to let me do it . . .

VERNON   (*He sits up*) Anyway, I think you and I have a major decision to make.

SONIA   I love major decisions.

VERNON   Tomorrow is Thursday. We can either try to work this weekend . . .

SONIA   Or?

VERNON   Or—a friend of mine has this beach house in Quogue.

SONIA   I choose or!

VERNON   Realizing, of course, that I have only the basest interests at heart.

SONIA   If you don't, we might as well work.

VERNON   We'll leave tonight. Avoid the maniacs. I'll pick you up in an hour. If you're five minutes late, walk toward the ocean and turn left.

SONIA   Vernon, are you as excited as I am?

VERNON   Naturally. But I'm the fella. I'm acting cool.
     (*He starts to go*)

SONIA   Hey! (*He stops*) I kiss on first dates. (*He crosses back and kisses her gently*) Are you always so gentle?

VERNON It's my classical training. I start with pianissimo and
build to full orchestra . . . I'll be back with thirty-eight guys
in tuxedos.
> (*He goes off*)

SONIA (*To herself*) All right, don't get yourself all worked up,
Sonia. You've been through all this before. (*She turns to go,
then stops*) But God, it sure is starting off *right!!*
> (*She sings "Right," backed up by her* VOICES)

Right
Ev'ry-thing about this feels right.
Ev'ry-thing is perfectly fine
At this minute and this time.
I'm finding that light
Shining on me lookin' so bright
Feelin' alive again
Makin' me sure that he's more than
All right for me.
I can hear those voices inside of me
Tellin' me my heart wouldn't lie to me.
If I were to say in a word
What I'm feelin' tonight I'd
Say—

GIRLS
Wrong, wrong, wrong
Oh, baby, it's wrong now.
Wrong, wrong, wrong
Gonna do it again now.
Don't make the same mistake twice.
Ooo—

SONIA
Don't need nobody's advice

GIRLS
But if you're gonna do it, baby,
You better do it right.

SONIA
I'm gonna do it right

GIRLS

Get it on

SONIA

Got so much to pack now

GIRLS

Get him hot

SONIA

I better wear black now

GIRLS

Go for it and let him see what
Heaven can be

SONIA

He's gonna find a lot of woman
In me

GIRLS

And me
Make this right, right, right

SONIA

Lookin' for fun now

GIRLS

Check him out

SONIA

This may be the one now

GIRLS

Get him, honey, while you can
Ooo—

SONIA

This could be my magic man

GIRLS

'Cuz if you're goin' for it, baby

SONIA

I'm gonna get it right

GIRLS
>You better get it right

SONIA
>I'm gonna get it right

GIRLS
>You better get it right
>You better get it right
>You better get it right.

SCENE 5

On the street.

A car drives up. VERNON *is in a green Austin, 1970 model. The top is down. He honks the horn, leaps out of the car, looks at his watch . . . then stops himself.*

VERNON   Okay, Vernon, buddy . . . Let's get a hold of ourselves. Let's examine what's going on here . . . We have either met ourselves one terrific woman . . . *or* . . . we are about to step blindly into the old poopy-doo once again! Caution! I suggest caution! Make no commitments . . . Make no promises . . . Make *whooppee* and then make a getaway! (*He starts to walk away.*) And yet—
    (SONIA *appears in "normal" clothes. She carries a bag and a tennis racket*)

SONIA   You're ten minutes late. I've been waiting in the lobby.

VERNON   I'm sorry. The car came unassembled. (*He reaches over and takes her bag*) A tennis racket? Who's going to have time for tennis?

SONIA   Shhh. It's for the neighbors.
    (*She gets into the car*)

VERNON   Those look like normal clothes. Where'd you get normal clothes?

SONIA   I have a friend who does Geritol commercials.

VERNON   (*Gets in the car*) Any misgivings or second thoughts before I blow two hundred bucks on gas?

SONIA   I am a fully committed woman.

VERNON   Good.

SONIA   I've never been to Quogue. What's it like?

VERNON   It's a fishing village founded by the Pilgrims in 1628. "Quogue" is an old Indian name.

SONIA   What does it mean?

44

VERNON   "Mess around on weekends."
   (*He starts the car. They drive off, singing "Right"*)

SONIA *and* VERNON
 Right, right
 Ev'rything about this feels right.
 Ev'rything is perfectly fine
 At this minute and this time.
 We're finding that light

VERNON
 Yeah! I can't remember feelin'
 This fine.

SONIA
 Did you say that to Natalie Klein?

VERNON   (*Speaks*) Sonia!

SONIA
 Hold me and tell me again.

SONIA *and* VERNON
 Tell me
 Just how sweet this weekend will be
 Just you and me
 Just you and me.
 Don't say a word
 Ev'rything's feelin' so right.
 Who'd ever thought we'd be here? Ooh!
 I can't wait 'till we get to Quogue.
 We still aren't there
 But we're sure doin' better than
 We've done before
 That's right.

SONIA
 Do do do do do do
 Do do
 Do do do do do do.

SCENE 6

On the road. They drive along, quietly.

SONIA You've been quiet a long time. What are you thinking about?

VERNON Oh . . . nothing. It's okay. I'll handle it.

SONIA Does it concern me?

VERNON Well, yes. In a way.

SONIA Well, if it concerns me, it's important. What is it?

VERNON We're lost.

SONIA I thought we were. I just thought you were going a new way.

VERNON I am. No one ever went this way before. I haven't seen a sign in English for hours. I think we're in Bangladesh.

SONIA (*Looks around*) You better pull off the road.
(*He pulls off the road. They come to a stop*)

VERNON I should have driven a piano. I'm safe behind a piano.

SONIA We'd better look for a gas station. I have to make a phone call, anyway.

VERNON Who are you calling?

SONIA I forgot to tell Leon I was going out of town. He promised he'd take care of my plants whenever I was gone.

VERNON I thought you sent Leon off to camp with the twelve-year-olds.

SONIA He's the only one who has a key. I don't want my plants to die.

VERNON So call the forest rangers! I don't understand you, Sonia. How can you call your ex-lover while you're spending the weekend with another guy?

SONIA He's not my ex-*lover*. He is a warm, intimate, personal friend that I'm not emotionally attached to any more . . . Just as I hope you're not a "guy I'm spending the weekend with." I don't spend weekends with *guys!*

VERNON Jesus, you really love to put a name tag on everything, don't you? You didn't happen to write "Look for the Union Label," did you?

SONIA What is there about our relationship that you hate to see take a turn for the better?

VERNON Talking! We're always talking about our relationship. Why don't we just have a relationship?

SONIA Okay! Fine! Now that I know the rules, you won't hear a peep out of me until Monday morning! Quogue, please!
(*She sits angrily. He tries to start the engine. It chokes but doesn't catch. He tries it again. No go. One more time and it dies*)

VERNON Now see what you did. You got the car upset. (*He gets out, slams the door, goes to the hood and lifts it up. He reaches inside and burns his finger. He winces and blows on it. He looks inside*) We burned our luggage! (*He looks around for help. To* SONIA) Do you know anything about engines? (*She looks away, doesn't answer*) May Day! May Day! We have to break radio silence here, we're in trouble. As I see it, we have two alternatives . . . A, we walk until we find a phone or a gas station, or B, we push the car until we get help.

SONIA Good thinking. I'll take A, you try B!
(*She takes her things out of the car and starts walking away. And she is gone . . . He kicks the tire out of anger and starts to push . . . accompanied by the male* VOICES, *singing "Right"*)

VERNON
Wrong!
Ev'ry-thing about this feels wrong.

God, I would give half my royalties
Just for a phone booth—
Maybe not half!

BOYS
  You're headed for trouble

VERNON
  I'd give a lot now

BOYS
  Let your fingers do the walkin'

VERNON
  Oh, so right

BOYS
  You better start dialin'

VERNON
  That's right now

BOYS
  You're headed for trouble. (BOYS *hand him a phone and exit*)
VERNON

  Thank you, boys.

VERNON (*Into phone*) Hello? . . . Automobile Club? . . . I
have a dead English sports car that's lying in state here . . .
Well, either a tow truck or a quick burial, that's up to you
. . . Yes, I am a member of the club. I even go to the meetings . . . Where? Well, it's either Long Island or the planet
Pluto. I haven't seen any earth people all night . . . Well, I
don't know much about engines, but I think it's the distributor. The *distributor*, the crook who sold me the car . . . I
don't *know* the exact location. The last sign I saw said, "Fresh
Clams, Four Dollars a Bucket." Does that help?

BOYS
  You're headed for trouble . . .

VERNON "Pepe's Foot-Long Hot Dogs," is that familiar?

BOYS

Trouble . . .

VERNON "Cocker Spaniel Puppies for Sale," you know that place?

BOYS

Trouble . . .

SCENE 7

Beach house in Quogue. We hear the surf pounding against the shore.

SONIA Hello? . . . Sonia Walsk . . . Any calls? . . . I'm in Quogue. The number is 516 653-0121 . . . but don't give it out to anyone . . . except, you know . . .

VERNON (*Enters with bags*) Vernon Gersch . . . noted composer . . . died at seven-twenty A.M. this morning. Vice-President and Mrs. Mondale will attend services.
(*He drops bags, falls onto bed*)

SONIA Listen, no more arguments. Let's just forget what happened. Come on. It's going to be a gorgeous day. Would you like to go for a dip?

VERNON (*Sits up*) A dip? Yes. Possibly you could rent a crane and have me lowered into the water a few times . . . like a tea bag.

SONIA Vernon . . . we can still salvage the rest of this weekend. If you drop the sarcasm, I'll drop the petulance. Except for the stinking miserable trip out here, I'm having a wonderful time. Come on, lazy. I'll race you to the beach.

VERNON Please, I don't wanna play Sandra Dee. (*Holds his back*) Ooh, the pain. The Austin is not an economical car. It only gets two miles to the push. (*He sits up, looks around*) Where are we?

SONIA (*Starts to fix her hair*) In Quogue. In your friend's house.

VERNON (*Gets up, looks around*) This isn't his house.

SONIA Of course it is. Two fifty-seven Sea View Road.

VERNON Two *sixty*-seven! *Sixty*-seven! How did you get in here?

SONIA The key didn't work, so I just *forced* it open.

VERNON (*Rushes to window, looks out*) That's the house! Next door . . . (*He grabs bags, groceries*) Jesus, breaking and entering, two to five years. Just when my career got going . . . Come on, will you?

SONIA Vernon! Let's stay here. I like this house much better than that one.

VERNON So does my friend, but he doesn't own this one . . . Hurry up, will you? And wipe off your fingerprints.

SONIA If we hear anyone, we'll run out the back way. Oh, Vernon, I can't think of anything more romantic than making love in a house you just broke into.

VERNON Really? How about making love in a house you can't get *out* of? Like a prison. Let's go, let's go.

SONIA It's the first time for us, Vernon. I want it to be special.

VERNON I do too. But I also want it to be legal . . . Will you get your things, and this time you push the car.

SONIA My God, Vernon, you are so—so—so *straight!*

VERNON *Me? Straight??* The man hasn't been *born* yet who's as neurotic as I am!! You've given me nothing but trouble since the moment I met you. And if I know you another fifty years, there isn't a day that'll go by where you won't drive me insane . . . And *still* I'm crazy nuts for you. So don't tell me about *straight!!*

SONIA Then bend a little for me, Vernon. Please. Can't you bend?

VERNON I've been bending since the Triboro Bridge.
(*She lies back on the bed. She raises her arms toward him. He doesn't make a move toward her . . . She sits back up*)

SONIA Come on . . . All right . . . The last thing I want to do is tie you down to anything . . . especially a bed. I'll get my things.

VERNON Wait a minute! (*She stops*) Stay there! Sex wins again. I'll put the bags in the next house. If I have to run, I'll have enough trouble with my zipper.

(He turns and goes with the bags. She runs and calls after him)

SONIA   Vernon! Bring back the pistachio nuts for afterward!
(She sings "Just for Tonight")
Just for today
Let me love you.
Just for tonight
I'll close my eyes
And when I open them
My world will be all right.
It couldn't hurt anyone
It wouldn't hurt anyone

Just for today
I want to hold you.
Just for tonight
You'll be my dream.
And when the mornin' comes to wake me
That's all right.
It couldn't hurt anyone
It wouldn't hurt anyone

Takin' just one more chance
Tryin' for some fun.

Up to now
My life's been too much said
Too little done.

Just for today
I'll be my feelings
And I know they'll lead me home
And if we both come back a little wiser
It couldn't hurt anyone
It wouldn't hurt anyone
It shouldn't hurt anyone

Just for tonight
Just for tonight.
(VERNON comes back in, breathless)

VERNON We better do this quickly. A couple of seagulls just spotted me. (*He removes his jacket and shoes and lies next to her on the bed. Telephone rings*) Oh, Jesus!

SONIA I'll get it.

VERNON What do you mean, you'll get it? It's for *them,* not us!

SONIA It could be for me.

VERNON What?

SONIA I didn't know it was the wrong house. I called my service and left this number.

VERNON You left this number??? Why?

SONIA I don't know why. Force of habit, I guess . . . If it's Leon, I'll call him back.
      (*She picks up phone receiver*)

VERNON Sonia! I want you to put that phone down! I want you to hang up! And I don't want you calling him back . . . not today . . . not ever.

SONIA Look, I'm sorry about today. It was stupid. But Leon is still my friend. I can't promise never to speak to him again. That's not fair of you, Vernon.

VERNON I didn't say it was fair. I said it's what I wanted . . . Eventually we all have to cut ourselves loose from the coatrack.

SONIA Look, I know I've got big trouble in that area. But if I do it when you want me to and not when I'm *able* to, it'll come back to haunt the both of us. It's happened to me before. When my father died, I was away in college and I never had a chance to say goodbye. I don't want any more unresolved relationships. Let me say goodbye in my own time . . . in my own way.

VERNON It's your life . . . You do it any way you want, Sonia. (*He picks up his own bag*) I'll be next door . . . It suddenly doesn't feel like the right time to be in the wrong house.

(*He turns and goes. She sits on the bed . . . then puts the phone to her ear*)

SONIA Hello? . . . Leon? . . . Listen, I'm sorry but—this is a bad time to talk . . . *No!* Don't call back later . . . Later is a bad time too . . . It's *always* going to be a bad time, Leon . . . I *do* want to be your friend . . . I just don't know how to do it without hurting someone else . . . You take care of yourself, you hear me? I'm really counting on you to be good to yourself . . . Well, if you won't say it, I'll say it for both of us . . . Goodbye, Leon.

(*She hangs up and sings "Just for Tonight"*)

I'll be my feelings
And I know they'll lead me home.

Okay, Vernon Gersch, if it's a relationship you want, get ready for the big time.

It couldn't hurt anyone
It wouldn't hurt anyone
It shouldn't hurt anyone.

(*Phone rings, continues ringing. She picks up her bag and runs off*)

Curtain

Act Two

VERNON's *living room. Four o'clock in the morning. The room is in semi-darkness.*

VERNON, *in pajamas and open robe, is pacing wearily. He calls out to the city.*

VERNON   *Sleep!* I can't sleep! (*He crosses to piano, where his portable tape recorder is. He turns it on and speaks into it*) Journal . . . Monday, four o'clock in the morning . . . Well, it's happened . . . Just as I feared . . . LOVE FINDS VERNON GERSCH! CUPID STRIKES DOWN JULLIARD GRADUATE . . . How do you like *them* apples, old faithful Panasonic tape recorder? . . . I have all the symptoms of a pubescent adolescent . . . I have gone from Mozart and Beethoven to ga-ga and goo-goo . . . That's what you get for not looking where you step . . . My greatest fear is that I will now have to adopt Leon . . . I've got to get some sleep . . . (*The doorbell rings*) Doorbell at four-oh-two . . . We know who that is, don't we?

(*He crosses, turns on lights, opens door.* SONIA *steps in*)

SONIA   (*Breathless and rapidly*) Don't get nervous, Vernon. I know it's four o'clock in the morning, but I had to see you. I hope I didn't wake you. Oh, God, I can't catch my breath. I'm hyperventilating. (*She does*) I'm a wreck. I'm a nervous wreck. I haven't slept all night. I don't know how you do it. (*Takes scarf off her head*) Do you like my hair? I just had it cut.

VERNON   Just *now?* You found an all-night Vidal Sassoon?

SONIA   No. Earlier tonight. Then I went home and took a hot bath, me and the girls did some work and then I went to bed. Then at one o'clock in the morning my doorbell rings. I go to the door, open it up and you'll never guess in a million years who was standing there.

VERNON   (*Thinks*) . . . I give up.

SONIA   Leon!

VERNON   Leon!! Of course! It never entered my mind. (*He rushes to the window, yells out and waves*) Hey, Leon! Welcome home! We really missed you, buddy.

SONIA   He doesn't have a dime to his name. He doesn't have a place to stay. He looked like he'd been in a terrible fight, and Leon can't fight. He's got these teeny little fists . . . I couldn't kick him out on the street. I'm sorry, Vernon, I just couldn't.

VERNON   *I* could. Call *me* next time, I'd *love* to do it! Jesus, I haven't got the energy to participate in this yo-yo triangle any more, Sonia. Another few weeks of this, I'll be broke and Leon and I will end up sharing *your* apartment.

SONIA   That's more or less along the lines I wanted to discuss. I will not discard Leon like yesterday's garbage. On the other hand, I can't stay there with him. Not after what happened to us this weekend . . . Therefore, I was going to suggest—

VERNON   Don't tell me! (*He runs across the room*) Don't tell me!
       (*He runs out the door. He comes back in carrying two of* SONIA's *suitcases*)

SONIA   You don't have to say yes. It's just a suggestion.

VERNON   Pearl Harbor was a suggestion. (*He puts down suitcases*) A girl with packed suitcases is a very intimidating thing, Sonia.

SONIA   I thought you might be pleased. I thought you might like the idea of my moving in with you. If nothing else, Vernon, I'd never be late again.

VERNON   I adjusted to it . . . I set all my clocks back.

SONIA   Listen, Vernon, I'm not asking you to take me in out of pity or charity. I'm not asking you to take care of me. I will pay for my room and board.

VERNON   With what?

SONIA   I was going to borrow money from you. You can take it out of my future royalties. And I will not leave my unwashed laundry in the bathroom.

VERNON By all rights, *Leon* should do our laundry. He's the only one not paying rent.

SONIA Does that mean yes, Vernon, because I feel an emotional sonic boom building up inside me and I don't want to crack your windows . . . and I'll be damned if I'm going to cry in an apartment I have not been invited to live in.

VERNON What do you want me to do, draw up a lease?

SONIA Can't you say it, damn it? I'll write it out for you. Just repeat after me: "Please, Sonia, won't you please—"

VERNON YES, I WANT YOU TO LIVE WITH ME. ALL RIGHT??

SONIA That's sweet of you to ask.

VERNON You don't wear jockey shorts, do you? I hate getting underwear confused.
(*They kiss*)

SONIA Do you know what I'm going to do now?

VERNON What?

SONIA I'm going out in the hall and get the rest of my things.

VERNON Sonia . . . (*She stops*) . . . I was going to ask you to move in tonight. It was going to be a surprise. I was going to go over myself while you were out, pack up your things and have your apartment recycled . . . I want to make you happy. I want to make you rich . . . I want you to wear dresses that have never appeared on any stage . . .
(SONIA *exits.* VERNON *plays piano and sings "When You're in My Arms."*
During the second chorus of the song, VERNON *sings while her* VOICES *help her move in and his help put her things away. They move in posters, potted plants, a bicycle, framed photos, a blender, and a grandfather clock . . .*
His apartment begins to take on a change of appearance . . .
In the third chorus of the song, she changes into her

nightgown, VERNON *into his pajamas. The male and fe-male* VOICES *continue backing them up in the song . . .*

    VERNON, *now in his pajamas, goes back to the piano, still noodling with the song.* SONIA *crosses to him, ready for bed.*

    The stage is now half the living room, half his bed-room. The passage of time is about three weeks)

VERNON

    When you're in my arms
    And I feel you close to me
    Life's what it's supposed to be.
    I'm in love
    And you are my song.

SONIA

    You're my melody
    You're every dream I locked away.

VERNON *and* SONIA

    My whole world came alive
    The day you walked into my life.
    You are my song.
    Sing it.
    Let ev'rybody know I found you.
    Let ev'rybody know I found that thing that people love to
        sing about.
    Tell them
    Tell them if they didn't hear by now
    Tell 'em how I found that feeling that I waited for.
    I've got the world and more
    When you're in my arms.

VERNON

    I wish I had the words to say

SONIA

    I'll give 'em to you ev'ryday

VERNON *and* SONIA

    Tonight you're in my arms

It feels good in your arms
Tonight you're in my arms.

GIRLS

When you're in love
The time keeps tickin'
But you got no time to see it go.

VERNON

I only got eyes for my sweet,
    sweet baby
So love's the only time I know.

VOICES (BOYS *and* GIRLS)

When you're in love
Your smile gets wider
You wear a kind of magic glow.
The clock on the wall,
Well, it don't matter at all
'Cause love's the only time
You know.
Somethin' so right 'bout lovin' together
Two hearts are better than one.
Good, good lovin' and sweet, sweet music
Sure makes wakin' up fun.
Sure feels good to be lovin' each other
Wonder why we waited so long.
Sonia and Vernon
The fire is burnin'
We got ourselves our own sweet song.

SONIA *and* VERNON	VOICES
When you're in my arms	In your arms
I see a world I've never	Never seen.
seen.	

VERNON

I never knew that trees were green
'Til you were in my arms.

ALL VOICES

You are my song

SONIA
　　Thank you
　　For helpin' give my life some order.

VERNON
　　But where'd you put my tape recorder?
　　I want to write how good I feel tonight.

VERNON *is at the piano.* SONIA *is getting ready for bed.*

VERNON   I'm still not sure about the middle eight bars . . . Listen to this again. Tell me what you think.
(*He continues playing. She slams the keyboard cover down*)

SONIA   No!!

VERNON   (*Just getting his fingers out in time*) Are you *crazy??* My fingers don't work unless they're attached.
(*He rubs them protectively*)

SONIA   (*She turns down bed covers*) It's one o'clock in the morning. I've had enough music today. I don't want to hear any more music, Vernon. Let's go to bed.

VERNON   That's what you said *last* night. Then you got into bed and turned on *music.*

SONIA   When *other* people write it, it's music. When *we* write it, it's working. I'm through working today.

VERNON   How come when we're in bed and they're playing one of your old songs, you *love* it?

SONIA   Because that's already *written.* Then it's music. When it's still unwritten, it's not music. It's *working!*

VERNON   (*He looks at her, then looks away, trying to figure out her logic*) I *detest* it when a ridiculously illogical statement like that makes complete sense to me!

SONIA   Vernon . . . we've been working every day and every night since I moved in here three weeks ago. I saw you more socially when I didn't live with you. I want to go out to dinner. I want to go to a movie. I want to see people on the street and what girls are wearing these days. I want to see what the rest of the world is doing.

VERNON (*Looks out window at street*) You can see from here. They're not doing much.

SONIA You know what just occurred to me? The piano is your Leon. Don't talk to *me* about letting go.

VERNON Never—*never*—refer to my piano as Leon! And the reason I've been working so much is because I never had so much fun working before . . . I *like* it when I look over and see you curled up in a chair with a scribbled pad on your lap and a pencil in your mouth—all chewed to pieces like a beaver got to it . . . I like it when you come over and touch the back of my neck when something I've written particularly pleases you . . . I can't find a good enough reason to go out when its so terrific at home.

SONIA (*Touched*) Well . . . you do the same thing to me.

VERNON I don't chew my piano.
(*They are both on the bed*)

SONIA No . . . but you get the most incredible look in your face when you're searching for those first four bars in a song. I just watch you and wonder, "What's going on in his mind now? What does he hear inside his head that the rest of us can't hear?" And then your eyes roll upward and your tongue comes out to the corner of your mouth . . .

VERNON I know that look. Usually I'm thinking about lunch.

SONIA What are you thinking about right this minute?

VERNON (*He looks at her, smiles*) How to get Natalie Klein's initials off the towels.

BOTH
   When you're in my arms

VERNON
   I wish I had the words somehow

SONIA
   Shh, not now

BOTH
> Tonight you're in my arms
> And you'll be wakin' up in my arms.

ALL VOICES
> When you're in my arms . . .

(He turns out bed lamp. Lights fade)

The bedroom.
The middle of the night.
The telephone rings . . . A pause. It rings again.
The light goes on over the bed. SONIA *looks aι the clock.*

SONIA   It's a quarter to three. (*It rings again*) Aren't you going to answer it?

VERNON   There's no one I want to talk to who calls at this hour. (*It rings again. He picks it up*) Hello? . . . Who's this? . . . I'm sorry, I can't understand you . . . Who did you want? . . . Who? . . . Is this Leon? . . . Figures.

SONIA   Oh, God!

.VERNON   (*Into phone*) No, not Mervyn. *Vernon!* . . . You know, you got a goddamn nerve!

SONIA   I'm sorry, Vernon.

VERNON   (*Into phone*) None of your business what we're doing. (*To* SONIA) He wants to know what we're doing.

SONIA   Don't tell him.

VERNON   (*Into phone*) Listen, *pal*, you know it's a quarter after three?

SONIA   It isn't. It's only a quarter of.

VERNON   (*Into phone*) Is that English? I don't know what the hell you're saying. (*To* SONIA) The man is either stoned or he's Greek. I can't understand him.

SONIA   (*Crossing over*) Let me speak to him.

VERNON   (*Handing her the phone*) He sounds like he's smoking one of your old dresses.

SONIA   (*Into phone*) Leon? . . . It's me . . . Are you all right?

VERNON   Why do you give him an unlisted number? My *mother* doesn't have this.

65

SONIA (*Into phone*) Leon, what's going on? . . . Are you alone? . . . You don't sound right to me . . .

VERNON Don't be nice to him! What are you being nice to him for?

SONIA (*Into phone*) What are you on, Leon? . . . You haven't done anything stupid, have you?

VERNON Hang up! It's my phone, I pay the bills. Hang up!

SONIA (*To* VERNON) Will you please stop! He's in trouble. (*Into phone*) Leon! I want you to lie down on the sofa and just close your eyes. I'm going to be there in ten minutes . . . Just hold on and wait for me, Leon. I'm on my way now. (*She hangs up*) I've got to get dressed. Could you please call downstairs and ask them to get me a cab?

VERNON Are you serious?

SONIA (*Getting dressed*) I've never heard him like this. He sounds manic. It's the last time, Vernon. I'll never go again, I swear. But I've got to go tonight.
(*She continues dressing*)

VERNON They have numbers you can call when you're in trouble. You dial "JUNKIE" or something.

SONIA Don't you understand? He doesn't want outside help. He wants *me*.

VERNON Funny, so do I. Maybe I should go in the other room and call this number.

SONIA I know what he's trying to do. I know how irrational he is. But somehow I just can't ignore it, knowing it's possible he just swallowed a bottle of pills.

VERNON He wouldn't be calling you if he was trying to kill himself. His plan is to do this at three o'clock every morning and kill *me*!
(SONIA *puts on colorful knitted leg warmers, takes* VERNON's *necktie from the bedstand and ties it around her waist, gathers up her nightgown to above her knees*

and tucks it under the tie. She then puts on shoes and a knee-length cape)

SONIA I'm sorry, Vernon, I just have to go. (*She is dressed, crosses to him*) I just want you to know, aside from everything else, I love you for being so patient with me . . . No matter what I put down on paper, I still haven't expressed the way I feel about you . . . And let's not go out tomorrow night. I like things just the way they are. I'll be back in a half-hour. Could you let me have five dollars for the cab?

VERNON (*Takes money off bureau*) You're going out like that? You look like you're going to the forest to visit your grandmother. (*He gives it to her. She kisses him quickly. And she is gone. Calls after her*) You'd better be back. We have a ten o'clock recording date in the morning. The demo, remember? I could understand all this if I were living with a doctor . . .

Recording studio. Music is heard.
We hear a telephone ring through the receiver, then a voice comes on . . .

WOMAN   Four-seven-one-six—Miss Walsk.

VERNON'S VOICE   (*Impatient*) Hello, four-seven-one-six. Is she there?

WOMAN   There's no answer. Can I take a message, please.

VERNON'S VOICE   It's Vernon Gersch again. Tell her I've called seventeen times. Tell her I've— No, never mind. Tell her to forget it. (*He hangs up angrily*) Cut the tape, Phil. Cut the tape. (*The track music cuts off.* VERNON *enters*) I called everywhere. I can't find her. How much longer can I hold the studio?

PHIL   (*Offstage*) Maybe another twenty minutes.

VERNON   Unless she's in a terrible accident, I'm gonna *kill* her! If she doesn't show in five minutes, I'll cut the tape myself.
(*He sits at piano as* SONIA *rushes in*)

SONIA   (*Breathless*) Don't say it! Whatever you're thinking, I agree with you. Only please don't say it.

VERNON   Sort of limits our conversation, doesn't it? Okay. How'd the Yankees do last night?

SONIA   Oh, God, maybe you'd better say it. Get it all out, because I deserve it.

VERNON   (*Furious*) I have been sitting here since— How do you have the nerve not to even— Do you realize what it feels like to— If you were a guy right now— I've said enough!

SONIA   It's all right. You're probably exhausted. Did you get any sleep at all?

VERNON   I was going to take a Valium but I couldn't get my teeth unclenched. (*Into mike*) Phil, are you ready to go?

PHIL (*Offstage*) I've been ready all morning.

VERNON Couldn't you call me? Or would dialing endanger Leon's life?

SONIA I *tried* to call you. But when I picked up the phone, he went berserk. He ripped the wire out of the wall.

VERNON I did too, but I have a plug-in phone.

SONIA He's leaving for California tonight. I don't think he'll ever bother us again.

VERNON *Certainly* he will. Only now he'll bother us three hours earlier . . . He will keep bothering us just as long as you keep taking his phone calls.

SONIA I will never take his phone call again, Vernon. That's a promise.

VERNON (*Looks at her . . . Pushes a sheet of music in front of her and takes out a pen*) Put it in writing!

SONIA I said *I promised!*

VERNON That's not good enough. I need proof I can read before I go to bed. I can't sleep with one eye on the phone and the other eye on you.

PHIL (*Offstage*) What do you say, Vernon? Time is running out.

VERNON (*Into mike*) For everybody. (*To* SONIA) Write it, Sonia. Please. I think it's important.

SONIA You're serious.

VERNON Deadly!

SONIA (*Glares at him, grabs the pen*) You want script or calligraphy?

VERNON You can write it in Latin for all I care. I'll get the druggist to translate.

SONIA (*Writes*) "I, Sonia Walsk, being of sound mind and body—"

69

VERNON You don't have to leave him to me in your will. Just say you won't take his calls.

SONIA (*Writes quickly*) "—will never take Leon Persky's calls again, so help me God!" Okay? Have you got a pen knife? We can each drop a little blood on it, make it binding.

VERNON (*Takes paper*) That won't be necessary.

SONIA Would you like to have it notarized? How about a witness to co-sign?

PHIL (*Offstage*) I can witness that.

VERNON (*Into mike*) Will you stay out of this, Phil! (*To* SONIA) Thank you. I appreciate this. It means a lot to me. (*Then he tears it up and throws it in the wastebasket*) Now maybe we can get on with our work. (*Into mike*) You can roll anytime, Phil. We're ready now.
    (*He sits at the piano*)

PHIL (*Offstage*) Rolling tape . . . take one . . . "I Still Believe in Love." Gersch and Walsk.
    (PHIL *plays the tape intro to the song,* VERNON *nods to* SONIA . . . *She begins to sing. But she is still so angry, she bites the words off sharply and bitterly. He stop playing*)

VERNON (*Into mike*) Cut it, Phil! Hold it! Wait a second! (*Turns to* SONIA) That's a little hostile, isn't it? This is a ballad, not the official Nazi party song.

SONIA It's a mood piece. This is the mood I'm in.

VERNON Yeah? Well, gloom isn't selling so well these days. Can we try it a little more cheerful? Say, in the key of happiness (*Into mike*) Okay, Phil.

PHIL (*Offstage*) Take two . . . "I Still Believe in Love" . . . Gersch and Walsk.
    (SONIA *glares at him*)

SONIA That was a lousy thing to make me do. Don't you ever do something like that to me again. I don't deserve that from anyone.

PHIL (*Offstage*) I don't have that in my lyric. Is that a new lyric, Vernon?

VERNON (*Into mike*) No. That's from life, Phil. Lyrics are with the music. (*To* SONIA) So far today it has cost me two hundred and forty dollars and all we've recorded is eight seconds of *vengeance*. Are we still on Leon? I'll write him into the song if that's the only way to get it on tape.

SONIA No. We're well past Leon. We're into *us* now. Sonia and Vernon! You wanted five songs, we've written five songs. Every day and every night for a month. I think we've got a hell of a collaboration going, but our relationship could use a little working on.

VERNON We're already living with each other, it's too late to start dating.

SONIA (*Suddenly nervous*) What's wrong, Vernon? Something is wrong when the dating was more fun than the living.

VERNON (*Turns away, soberly*) I don't know . . . I can't seem to get it straight in my mind. Am I living with the girl I work with, or working with the girl I live with?

SONIA I didn't know there was a difference.

VERNON Try "enormous" . . . I don't know which Sonia it is I'm so angry with right now. Which one do I complain to when the other one is driving me berserk?

SONIA Funny, but I've never thought of *you* as two people. And if I did, I would feel the same about both of them.

VERNON Well, you're much more liberal-minded than me. I'm just one of those old-fashioned monogamists . . . Are you hungry? I'm starved. (*Into mike*) Phil, is there any coffee and Danish left in there?

PHIL (*Offstage*) There's one Danish, but I've been using it as an ashtray.

SONIA Oh, God. I have that nervous feeling in my stomach you get when someone you care for is about to tell you something you don't care for.

VERNON Not at ninety dollars an hour. Let's make the tape.

SONIA (*Snaps at him*) *I'll pay for the goddamn tape.* Talk to me, Vernon. I'm here. Live! I don't want to be something you can erase when you get home.

VERNON (*Thinks*) I don't know . . . I've said it all . . . I think between you and me and me and you, we have one relationship too many.

SONIA Jesus, Vernon, do you expect me to split myself down the middle and offer you the part of your choice? I am a fairly attractive, intelligent, twentieth-century woman, not, I pray to God, a broiled lobster. I am an entity. I come all assembled and complete. I work, walk, talk, make love and drive some people berserk. I am Sonia Walsk. Leave out the battery and you can play with me all you want, but the eyes won't light up.

VERNON Wait a minute. When I'm not at the piano, I'm just of average intelligence. Speak slowly, like I'm from Norway. I didn't get all of that. I didn't get *any* of that.

SONIA I'm just asking you to be patient with me. If not, let's say goodbye now. I can't go through another one of those lingering five-year breakups.

VERNON What you ask for, Sonia, isn't unreasonable.

SONIA Well, that's encouraging.

VERNON I just don't know if it's possible.

SONIA All right . . . You want to try one me at a time? Okay! I can find someone else to work with. I've done it before. I'll get rid of my pads and pencils tonight. I can use the drawer space, anyway.

VERNON It's not going to work, Sonia.

SONIA (*Near tears*) Why not? You care for me, Vernon, I know that. What in God's name is it you're afraid of?

VERNON Everything! I feel so damned threatened by you. I don't have your patience, your understanding, your incredible gift for still caring and worrying about a man that you no longer care or worry about. You're an emotional Florence Nightingale, and I don't know if I can measure up to your standards.

SONIA Are we talking about the same person? You're the one I look up to with respect and admiration.

VERNON You want the God's honest truth, Sonia? You scare the hell out of me. I feel so competitive with you. When you tell me the last eight bars are no good, I want to quit the business and go back to Juilliard for another four years . . . Because I am so confused by you, I keep forgetting who *I* am . . .

SONIA (*Softly*) Ask me. I'll tell you.

VERNON I'd rather find out for myself.

SONIA (*Nods*) I understand . . .

VERNON I'm sorry, Sonia.

SONIA What the hell. I'm sure we'll both get a couple of good songs out of this . . . I'll get my things out tonight.

VERNON Oh, a package came for you this morning. From the Hanna Theater in Cleveland.

SONIA That'll be my gown from the *Rocky Horror Show*.

VERNON I will miss the Broadway melody in your closet. You still feel like cutting the demo? I've got the track laid down. Phil's all ready to go.

SONIA Sure. Why not? Might as well have a souvenir to take home.

VERNON I'll listen to it in the booth.
(*He starts out*)

SONIA (*Nervously*) You're not leaving without saying goodbye, are you?

VERNON No . . . I will definitely say goodbye. That's a promise.
(*He goes. She sits on the stool and signals to* PHIL *she is ready*)

PHIL (*Offstage*) Take three . . . "I Still Believe in Love" . . .
Gersch and Walsk.

    (*We hear the musical intro and she sings "I Still Believe
in Love"*)

SONIA

    After all the tears I cried
    You'd think I would give up on love
    Get off this line.
    But maybe I might
    Get it right this time.

    I was there as passion turned to pain
    Sunshine turned to rainy days.
    Yet here I am
    Ready to begin once again.

    All my life I've been a dreamer
    Dreamin' dreams that always broke in two.
    But I still believe in love
    And I love believin'
    Maybe you can make my dreams come true.

    Here content with who I am
    I'm reachin' out my hand to him
    Once again.
    At least I know I made myself a friend.

    All my life I've been a dreamer
    Dreamin' dreams that never quite came true
    But I still believe in love
    And I love believin'
    I'll keep on dreamin'
    Because I still believe in love
    I still believe in love and me and you.
    I still believe in love . . .

VERNON (*Offstage, over mike from the booth*) That was nice,
Sonia . . . Thanks a lot . . . I'll, er . . . see you around.

SONIA Yeah? When?

VERNON   (*Offstage*) I don't know . . . I think I'm going to get out of New York for a while.

SONIA   Oh . . . Well, try not to get lost.

VERNON   (*Offstage*) Goodbye, Sonia.

SONIA   Gee . . . you kept your promise. Goodbye, Vernon . . . Phil? Would you play that back for me? I feel like hearing a familiar voice.

    (PHIL *plays back the beginning of the song*)

SONIA'S VOICE

    After all the tears I cried
    You'd think I would give up on love
    Get off this line
    But maybe I might get it right this time . . .

    (*We go to dark, the song continues . . . We hear the* VOICE *of Johnny Mathis . . .*)

VOICE

    All my life I've been a dreamer
    Dreamin' dreams that never quite came true
    But I still . . .

    (*We hear the* VOICE *of a disc jockey*)

VOICE   That was Johnny Mathis and "I Still Believe in Love." Twelve weeks on the charts, and this week number two.

Fade Out

VOICE   (*In the scene change*) Dr. Edwards . . . Dr. Lionel Edwards, please check with the admitting office. Dr. Edwards, please . . .

SCENE 5

A hospital room. Late afternoon a few months later.

VERNON *is lying in bed in a hospital gown. His leg is in a cast. He is on the phone.*

VERNON (*Into phone*) Two-thirty in the afternoon . . . Crossing Sunset Boulevard. It said "walk," so I walked. Then it must have said "hit" because I got hit . . . a '72 Pinto with no issurance. Ten thousand Rolls Royces in Beverly Hills and I get hit by an unemployed Mexican gardener with a sweet face . . . Well, I was going to fly back to New York Monday, but I'm not going unless I can take my leg . . . Listen, Lou, I'll talk to you later. They're taking me upstairs now for tap-dancing lessons . . . 'Bye. (*He hangs up. He picks up his tape recorder, presses on button and talks into mike*) Journal. January 16. Cedars Sinai Hospital. Los Angeles. They brought me fish for lunch today. I think they caught it in the intensive care ward. I am tied down to this bed in a marvel of medical science that was once used to get people to talk during the Spanish Inquisition. It makes going to the bathroom in the middle of the night the greatest adventure of my life. I thought of calling Sonia today. Oh, well. It was just a thought. (*There is a knock on the door*) Come in.

> (*He turns off recorder.* SONIA *comes in carrying a gift-wrapped box*)

SONIA Hi! Volunteer song lady. Need any books, magazines, lyrical ideas?

VERNON Next to a waiter from the Stage Delicatessen, there is *no one* I'd rather see.

SONIA I'm still showing up late. I just heard about it this morning. I read it in the daily *Variety*.

VERNON Oh, good. Two breaks in one week. I heard you were in California. Doing your own album, someone said.

SONIA Yes. With Eclectic Records. Mark Rossetti's producing it.

VERNON   The best in the business. You look terrific. How does it
feel, wearing firsthand clothes?

SONIA   They itch. I heard you were in Europe.

VERNON   Yes. Paris, for two months. Scoring the Louis Malle
picture.

SONIA   How'd you like it?

VERNON   I had a little trouble with the language. Every time I
ordered breakfast, they'd bring me a bicycle.

SONIA   This is really amazing, because I was on my way here
this morning, anyway. I was going up to the fifth floor to visit
—a friend.

VERNON   Don't tell me! Leon! (*She nods*) *Fan*-tastic! I knew
we'd end up living together. Just out of curiosity, Leon doesn't
drive a '72 Pinto, does he?

SONIA   No. He's in for some tests. They're not crazy about his
white-cell count.

VERNON   I kept hearing the phone ring outside at two o'clock in
the morning. Now I know who it was. I hope it's nothing serious.

SONIA   I hope so too.

VERNON   You're never going to let go of that responsibility, are
you?

SONIA   I haven't seen him in three months. I think I'm making
headway.

VERNON   Maybe I'll hobble up there one afternoon. I've always
wanted to see what the Masked Stranger looked like . . .
Where are you living?

SONIA   Mark has a house in Beverly Hills. I'm staying in the
guest cottage.

VERNON   I have a place out at the beach.

SONIA   I thought you couldn't swim.

VERNON   Well, it's not *in* the water. It's back a little . . . I met a
terrific girl jogging on the beach. We have a good relationship.
She runs home every night.

SONIA   Saves the hassle of packing and unpacking.

VERNON   I sure miss the crispness of our conversations.

SONIA   I'll leave you one. You can put it in the freezer . . . Oh,
I almost forgot. This is for you.
(*She puts the box on the table*)

VERNON   Oh, that's very sweet. Put it on the bed. I'll break it
open with my leg.

SONIA   (*Starts to untie ribbon*) Just to keep your mind occu-
pied. (*She lifts off the cover and takes out a toy, a miniature
piano, one that really plays. She hands it to him*) It's a Steinway grand. Someone left it out in the rain.

VERNON   I love it. (*He hits a few keys*) Perfect for writing "The
Minute Waltz" . . . It's very thoughtful of you.

SONIA   True. I've thought of you a lot.
(*They look at each other . . . then she turns away*)

VERNON   I'm really glad you dropped by, Sonia.

SONIA   It was nice of you to break a leg so I'd have a reason.

VERNON   Right. Now I know how to get in touch with you.

SONIA   Well, I've got to run.

VERNON   I wish I could.

SONIA   (*Extends hand*) Goodbye, Vernon.

VERNON   (*Shakes it warmly*) Goodbye, Sonia.

SONIA   Take care of yourself.

VERNON   If not me, who then?

SONIA   I don't know. Why don't you give it some thought?
(*She looks at him as though she were about to say more
. . . then changes her mind and goes. He looks down at*

*the small piano and tinkers with it. He begins to play
. . .* VERNON *sings "Fill in the Words." And there singing
along with him appear his three* VOICES, *all in hospital
gowns*)

VERNON

You play a "C"
You get a "C."
That's simple
That's easy
But there was you
There was me.
Not so simple
Not easy.

I'm never quite able to say what I feel.
I know that sounds absurd.
The only way you can hear me is to listen to my
 song without words.
 (*He plays*)
That's what I'm feelin' right now
And I'm writing this love song for you to
Fill in the words.
You were ev'rything good
I know you loved me.
I just couldn't make us work out
And all I could do was leave it to you
To fill in the words.

VERNON *and* BOYS

Fill in the words

VERNON	BOYS
If I had the words	Ah—

I'd have a song
And maybe it would tell
me where I belong.
With you I had the words
 for free.
It's just in lovin' you
I was losin' me.

79

I'm hopin' you'll un-
  derstand
That until I can find
those words for my-
  self
Will you fill in the words?

VERNON *and* BOYS
  Fill in the words

VERNON	BOYS
If I had the words	If I had the words
I'd have a song	I'd have a song
And maybe it would tell	
me	Maybe—tell me
Where I belong.	Where I belong.
With you and me I wasn't	
sure.	Ah—
Was I less?	
Were you more?	
I'm hopin' you give me	
some time	
And if that kid on the	
coatrack	
Wants to come back,	
Wants one more try,	
Where will you be?	
Will you still fill in the	
words?	
Will you	Ah—
Fill in the words?	
	Ah—Ah.

SCENE 6

Her New York apartment. A few months later. About ten in
the evening.
It is winter. The apartment is dark. The phone rings.
She opens the door and enters. She crosses to the phone.

SONIA Hello? . . . Oh, hi . . . No, I was just out walking in
the snow . . . How are you, Leon? . . . Well, you *sound* better . . . When did you check out? . . . You what? . . . You're
worried about *me?* . . . That's a switch . . . Well, don't. I'm
terrific . . . You got a job? Where? . . . Oh, that's wonderful
. . . Leon, you don't have to pay me back anything . . . That's
what old friends are for . . . Okay. Ten dollars a week for
forty years . . . You know, we may not have had the
healthiest relationship in the world, but at least it's reliable
. . . I wish you the best of everything, Leon . . . I know you
do . . . (*The doorbell rings*) Goodbye.
(*She hangs up, crosses to door, turns on lights and opens*
door. VERNON *stands there with winter coat, collar up,*
gloves and cap with snow on it, leaning on a cane)

VERNON Do you know I've waited my whole life to do this?

SONIA To do what?

VERNON Appear at the door with my coat collar up, snow in my
hair, carrying a cane and walking with a limp. Tyrone Power
in *A Yank in the R.A.F.*

SONIA And who am I?

VERNON Betty Grable.

SONIA Go out and pick another picture. I want to be Gene
Tierney. (*He turns and starts to go*) No. I'm kidding . . . Oh,
God, Vernon, I'm glad to see you.

VERNON The doctors said I'm allowed to hug now.
(*They embrace warmly*)

SONIA What are you doing in New York? Isn't your picture
opening in L.A. this week?

VERNON Tomorrow night. I can catch the noon plane . . . It was important I see you quickly. In another couple of days, I won't be limping any more . . . I would love a drink.

SONIA So would I. Anything special?

VERNON Oh. Claret. Madeira. Anything that looks good with a coat collar up.
(*She pours a drink and hands it to him*)

SONIA Our timing's getting better. If you rang the doorbell two minutes sooner, you would have caught Leon again.

VERNON Too bad. I would have said hello . . . We finally became buddies.

SONIA You met him?

VERNON Last week in the hospital. We took X-rays together. We were hoping you were there. We wanted a family portrait.

SONIA You know, for someone you never met, we sure spent a lot of time together . . . What'd you think of him?

VERNON Well, he was a lot better-looking than I'd hoped he'd be . . . He was actually quite witty and charming, which I found irritating as hell . . .

SONIA What did you talk about?

VERNON Well, I was very frank. I said, "Leon, old buddy, for a long time you've been a genuine pain in the ass to me" . . . And he looked at me and said, "Well, I guess there's got to be a Leon in everyone's life" . . . He said he was living with a girl now, and that if I wanted, I could call *him* at three o'clock in the morning.

SONIA That's my Leon.

VERNON He also told me what it was like growing up in Ithaca. Said it wasn't really worth the trouble. He told me how he met you at school. What you were like. He even remembered what you wore that first day he saw you running across the campus.

SONIA I can't remember. What was it?

VERNON   A naval officer's uniform.

SONIA   Of course. *Mister Roberts*. I was late for dress rehearsal.

VERNON   So that's how it started . . . When he checked out, he came down and we shook hands and said goodbye . . . And the last thing he said to me was . . . "Take care of our girl."

SONIA   (*A little embarrassed*) Leave it to Leon.

VERNON   Moving on to more mundane things, I hear your album's going to be very big. What's it feel like to finally have money?

SONIA   Old habits are hard to break. I flew home on economy.

VERNON   Well, now you can live it up. Get yourself a whole new wardrobe. Like all the costumes from *Annie*.

SONIA   Can I ask you a question, Vernon?

VERNON   Sure.

SONIA   What's wrong with us?

VERNON   Nothing. We're perfect. Well, *you're* perfect. I'm going to be perfect in eight months. I've been seeing a new therapist. A big, buxom, mother-earth analyst. When you break down and cry, she holds you in her arms and gives you cookies.

SONIA   I think that's terrific. What made you go back?

VERNON   Leon, probably. When I saw him walking out of my room looking happier than I was, I said to myself, "Vernon, I think it's time to pull into your friendly therapist for a thirty-four-year-old tune-up."

SONIA   You seem different, Vernon. I feel as though we're meeting for the first time. Does it seem like the first time to you?

VERNON   I don't know. Go out and come in twenty minutes late.

SONIA   I've gone through some changes myself. I've moved out of Mark's house . . . with no guilt, no sense of responsibility . . . I'm all alone for the first time in my life, handling it great and really proud of myself. In fact, tomorrow night I'm taking me out to dinner.

VERNON   I wish I was staying on. I was going to take myself out too. The four of us could have double-dated. (*They look at each other . . . an awkward pause*) I'd better go. Promise you'll go to the window and watch me limp away in the snow.

SONIA   With one hand holding back the curtains. A perfect Gene Tierney ending.

VERNON   (*Reaches in his pocket*) I thought it would be nice if we heard my love theme as I walked off. (*Hands her a cassette*) Would you put this cassette on as I get to the door?

SONIA   You actually had it recorded?

VERNON   Just eighteen pieces. No brass . . . I wrote it in the hospital . . . It's about you and me and Leon . . . I call it "You and Me and Leon"!

SONIA   (*Looks at cassette*) I like it better than the one you erased. "Rhapsody in Blue Cross."

VERNON   Everything good takes time . . . Goodbye, Sonia.

SONIA   Goodbye, Vernon.
(*He turns and limps to the door, opens it*)

VERNON   When you see me on the corner of Eighth Avenue, turn up the last eight bars. I want a big finish.

SONIA   Good luck with the opening. I'll call you from London, see how it went.

VERNON   You're going to London?

SONIA   Tomorrow. There's a boy there they say is the new Elton John. He wants me to write with him.

VERNON   Oh . . . well, you should love that. You'll get to wear things from *Private Lives* . . . Chin up and all that. (*He turns and goes. She puts on the cassette. We hear full orchestra play his "theme" . . . She crosses to the window. A perfect Gene*

Tierney ending . . . Her doorbell rings. She rushes to door and opens it. VERNON *stands there*) I can't get home. I lost my cane!

SONIA   What?

VERNON   There was snow on the ground. I stepped off the curb, leaned on my cane, and it went right down a sewer!
(*He leans against the door*)

SONIA   Are you all right?

VERNON   I couldn't walk. I had to crawl back here on my hands and knees. People passed by and dropped me a dollar-thirty in change . . .
(*She crosses to him*)

SONIA   We'll get you to the sofa.
(*He puts his arm around her. They get to sofa*)

VERNON   Can you imagine, on my hands and knees? A big dog came over and sniffed me, wondering what breed I was.

SONIA   Let me get the boy next door. He's an intern. He'll take a look at your leg.
(*She rushes out the door*)

VERNON   *Nooo!!!*
(*But she is gone. He sits there, a pained expression on his face . . . A moment passes, and she walks back in deliberately . . . holding his cane. She looks at him*)

SONIA   Look how much your cane loves you. It followed you all the way back to the door.

VERNON   (*Shrugs*) So I tried sympathy. I didn't know any other way to stop you.

SONIA   From what?

VERNON   From going to London. Why would you want to write with the new Elton John when you can write with the new Vernon Gersch?

SONIA   What happened to the *old* Vernon Gersch?

VERNON He didn't work out. He was driving me crazy. He wasn't sleeping at nights. He was coming late for appointments. He was writing and not enjoying it for the first time in his life . . . Oh, damn it, Sonia, come back! I've grown accustomed to your soul.

SONIA What makes you think we won't have the same problems as last time?

VERNON Because I've changed. I'm different. We'll have all *new* problems this time.

SONIA What happens if Mark Rossetti calls me in the middle of the night?

VERNON We'll change our schedule. We'll sleep during the day.

SONIA What happened to how difficult it is to work with some one you're living with?

VERNON We'll deal with it. Reasonably. Rationally. Intelligently . . . And I'll try to do the same.

SONIA It's going to be hard, Vernon.

VERNON Maybe impossible.

SONIA Things don't change overnight. It needs time.

VERNON Then why are we wasting any?

SONIA It needs commitment.

VERNON I'm ready to be committed right now.

SONIA No ego problems. No jealousies. No competitiveness. We each reserve the right to criticize the other's work without being accused of chauvinism or male domination.

VERNON I won't even notice you're a woman until lights out. Then it's every man for himself.

SONIA Well . . . London is cold now, anyway . . . Sure, let's give it a try. Hi. Sonia Walsk.

VERNON Yes. We met. I analyzed you once.

SONIA I thought you died.

VERNON No, that was Tannenbaum.

SONIA Oh, yes . . . So what'll it be? Your place tomorrow at ten?

VERNON I think I'd better spend the night here. There's ice out there and I don't have chains on my cane.

SONIA I'm glad you said that, Vernon. Because if you started for that door, I would have broken your other leg.

VERNON I am absolutely nuts for you, Sonia.

SONIA Not Sonia. Ingrid.

VERNON Ingrid?

SONIA (*The way he had said it*) I'm so lucky.
(*She throws her arms around him. Music swells*)

Curtain

About the Authors

Since 1960, a Broadway season without a Neil Simon comedy or musical has been a rare one. His first play was *Come Blow Your Horn*, followed by the musical *Little Me*. During the 1966–67 season, *Barefoot in the Park*, *The Odd Couple*, *Sweet Charity* and *The Star-Spangled Girl* were all running simultaneously; in the 1970–71 season, Broadway theatergoers had their choice of *Plaza Suite*, *Last of the Red Hot Lovers* and *Promises, Promises*. Next came *The Gingerbread Lady*, *The Prisoner of Second Avenue*, *The Sunshine Boys*, *The Good Doctor*, *God's Favorite*, *California Suite*, *Chapter Two* and the new musical hit, *They're Playing Our Song*.

Mr. Simon began his writing career in television, writing *The Sgt. Bilko Show* and Sid Caesar's *Your Show of Shows*. He has also written for the screen: the adaptions of *Barefoot in the Park*, *The Odd Couple*, *Plaza Suite*, *The Prisoner of Second Avenue*, *The Sunshine Boys*, *California Suite*, and most recently, *Chapter Two*. Other original screenplays he has written include *The Out-of-Towners*, *The Heartbreak Kid*, *Murder by Death*, *The Goodbye Girl* and *The Cheap Detective*. *Chapter Two* is now in production.

The author lives in California and New York with his actress wife, Marsha Mason. He has two daughters, Ellen and Nancy.

MARVIN HAMLISCH (Composer) is a graduate of the Juilliard School of Music and Queens College. In 1974, he received three Academy Awards: Best Song and Best Score for the motion picture *The Way We Were*, as well as Best Adaptation for his work on *The Sting*. Carole Bayer Sager and Marvin Hamlisch first collaborated on "Nobody Does It Better," the theme from *The Spy Who Loved Me*, for which they were nominated for an Academy Award. Mr. Hamlisch is the composer of *A Chorus Line*, for which he received the 1976 Tony Award.

CAROLE BAYER SAGER (Lyricist) graduated from New York City's High School of Music and Art and New York University. She has the distinction of having written lyrics for number-one songs in every area of popular music and has combined her words with the music of today's finest composers. Peter Allen, Marvin Hamlisch, Alice Cooper, Melissa Manchester, Bette Midler, Bruce Roberts, and Neil Sedaka, to name a few, have collaborated with Ms. Sager to create a string of hits that includes "Nobody Does It Better," "Midnight Blue," "I'd Rather Leave While I'm in Love," "Don't Cry Out Loud," and "A Groovy Kind of Love." Her songs have been recorded by artists as diverse as Aretha Franklin, Liza Minnelli, the Captain and Tenille, Judy Collins, Johnny Mathis, Carly Simon, Dolly Parton, and Frank Sinatra.